Stranger on the Shore

Stranger on the Shore

A SHORT HISTORY OF GRANTON

JAMES GRACIE

SecondSite Property

First published in 2003 by
Argyll Publishing
Glendaruel
Argyll PA22 3AE
Scotland
www.skoobe.biz

**British Library Cataloguing-in-
Publication Data.
A catalogue record for this book is
available from the British Library.**

ISBN 1 902831 53 5

Origination: Cordfall Ltd, Glasgow

Printing: Cromwell Press Ltd, Wiltshire

This book is dedicated
to the people of Granton

Foreword

THE RT HON ERIC MILLIGAN
LORD PROVOST OF THE CITY OF EDINBURGH

The Granton area of Edinburgh has a long and varied history from prehistoric and Roman times to the present day when the whole area along Edinburgh's waterfront is undergoing a dramatic transformation. To my knowledge no detailed history of the area has ever been written and this short history by James Gracie is most welcome.

By following the development of the area from its earliest records to the present time, we can see quite clearly how the development of Granton has been closely associated with the capital city of Edinburgh of which it has been a part since 1900.

Granton provided employment to many people from all over the city through the successful industries that sprang up there at the time of the Industrial Revolution. For many years, its thriving port ensured that Edinburgh could trade overseas and contributed to the city's prosperity. However, as many of the local industries went out of business and as the port became less suitable for modern day requirements, Granton went into a period of decline towards the end of the twentieth century.

At the time of writing exciting new plans are being progressed to develop the whole of Edinburgh's waterfront. Granton lies at the heart of these plans and in the next few years we look forward to the area once again becoming a vibrant, thriving community, an essential part of our new waterfront quarter.

I would like to congratulate James Gracie and all those who assisted him in pulling together the information he needed to write this book. It will be an important reference book for all those with an interest in the area and it will no doubt jog the memories of many local people.

Foreword

THE DUKE OF BUCCLEUCH & QUEENSBERRY KT VRD

Ever since the age of 11 in 1935 I have had a deep sense of affection and concern for Granton and its harbour. My parents took me to the Middle Pier for the Stone Laying ceremony in celebration of the centenary of its creation by my great-great-grandfather. This was as indelibly printed on my mind as the lettering on the stone.

However it was only after four years war service with the Royal Navy that I became associated with the management of the harbour itself and the development of the estate, once attached to Caroline Park which came into my family some three hundred years earlier.

As the Director most closely involved with Granton Harbour Ltd, I was always struck by the wonderful atmosphere of family loyalty and affection resulting from several generations of all our families working closely together.

I was greatly saddened to see this thriving little port with a community of 84 fine people close down, but I am delighted that the efforts of the Waterfront Edinburgh Project will once again bring life to this wonderful part of Edinburgh.

Now, 35 years after later, I would warmly welcome contact with any old friends from these happy and active years.

Contents

Introduction   11
Before 1800   17
    The Early Years   17
    The Medieval Period
        The Rough Wooing
        The Lands of Pilton
        Newhaven and the Great Michael
    Granton Castle   21
    Caroline Park   24
        The Gowrie Plot
        Viscount Tarbat
        Duke of Argyll
        The Dukes of Buccleuch
        Sir James Oughton
        The Industrial Revolution
After 1800   29
    The Buccleuch Family   30
    Caroline Park   32
        Lord Cockburn
        Lady Scott and 'Annie Laurie'
        AB Fleming
        Andrew and Birgitta Parnell
    Granton House   38
    Granton Harbour   41
        The Beginnings of the Harbour
        The Central Pier
        The Breakwaters
        The West Pier
        The Beginning of the twentieth Century
        World War I

World War II

After the War

The Fishing Fleet

Esparto Grass

Oil and Petroleum

Ferries

HMS Claverhouse

The Yacht Clubs

The Railways   65

Edinburgh, Leith and Newhaven Railway

Caledonian Railway

The Trams   69

Industries   73

Granton Quarry

Granton Gasworks

Madelvic Motors

Northern Lighthouse Board

United Wire

ABFleming

Caroline Park Foundry

Ferranti

Bruce Peebles

Other Industries

Granton Township   93

Life in Granton   97

Literary and Artistic Associations

National Museum of Scotland

National Gallery of Scotland

Housing Schemes

The Churches

The Schools

Edinburgh City FC

Waterfront Edinburgh   118

Index   125

Acknowledgements

This book could not have been written without the help and encouragement of many people. So many, in fact, that it would be impossible to name them all. But I must mention Christine Cook of Waterfront Edinburgh for overseeing the whole project and keeping cheerful while reading the emails I was forever sending her; Alan McGuinness of Proscot Public Relations, who recommended me for the job in the first place; Ian Moore, local historian, who has amassed a wealth of information and photographs about the area, and who kindly placed his considerable archives at my disposal; Andrew Boath of the Granton History Group for all the vital information he gave on where to begin my researches; Birgitta Parnell of Caroline Park, who gave me much valuable information on the history of Granton's oldest building; Pat Connor of Historic Scotland for information on Granton's listed buildings; Jessie Denholm for checking the sections on the railways, and saving my blushes by putting me right on several points; Cllr Elizabeth Maginnis of Edinburgh City Council for her encyclopaedic knowledge of the area, especially in the history of its housing and schools; the head teachers and staff of the area's schools for further information on education in Granton; Martin Ayres of North Edinburgh Arts for information on the arts in Granton; Darney Devlin for helping me research Granton's fishing fleet; Graeme Somner of Christchurch, Dorset, for allowing me to use material he has collected on Thomas Leishman Devlin, founder of the fishing fleet that bore his name; Graham Russell, Commodore of the Forth Corinthian Yacht Club for his help in researching the yachting clubs in Granton; Diane Robertson of the University Marine Biological Station on Cumbrae for details of Granton Marine Station; James Holloway of the National Galleries of Scotland and William Antony of the National Museums of Scotland for information on their organisations' presence in Granton; John and Alec Smith, market gardeners, who gave me much general information on Caroline Park and Granton Ice Works, and showed me all that is left of Granton Castle; His Grace The Duke of Buccleuch for information on the building of Granton Harbour and its subsequent history, as well as personal anecdotes about his experiences in the area; Mr N.A.G. Waugh, factor to the Buccleuch Estates, who supplied information on the history of the Dukes of Buccleuch; Tom Ward of Transco, who guided me through the history of Granton Gasworks; Iain Auld of Telford College for supplying information on the college's history; Stewart Bates and Terry Smith of Forth Ports, who supplied everything I needed to know about the building and subsequent history of Granton Harbour; Lorna Hunter of the Northern Lighthouse Board for sending me information on the board's one-time presence in Granton; the clergymen, clergywomen and church officers of Granton, who gave me information on ecclesiastical matters; Clifford and Ian Lutton for going over drafts and supplying much useful information and suggestions.

And also my wife, for enduring lengthy periods of enforced loneliness as I engaged in research, and then supplying endless cups of coffee and large Kit Kats as I sat before my word processor struggling to get the words onto the screen.

All played their part in bringing this book to fruition. However, if there are any errors or serious omissions within its pages, they are mine and mine alone.

JAMES GRACIE
FEBRUARY 2003

Introduction

I had thought, when I began, that this history of Granton would be a simple affair, taking up no more than twenty or so pages. Within a few days of starting my research, I was disabused of this notion. The place teemed with history, and I felt a strange elation at the discovery, even though it would involve me in more work than I had envisaged.

This stone carving of the unique drive wheel design still stands above the doorway of the former offices of the Madelvic car factory

It is true that I was dragged down many obscure avenues, only to return empty-handed. A BBC radio transmitter mast for the Third Programme, for instance; an underwater cable of some kind which connected Granton and Fife. What was the cable for? Electricity? The telephone? I have no idea. Details of these and other developments in Granton are hard to come by, and so I leave it to someone with more time to research subjects like these fully.

For this reason this book is by no means the last word. It is a popular history that seeks to inform and entertain, and perhaps awaken a few dormant memories.

But a definition is appropriate at this point. What exactly is 'Granton'? What area does it encompass? There is no definite answer, of course. But for purposes of this book, I had to come up with one. If you disagree with it I won't be offended. My area's eastern edge is Granton Road, its western edge is Pennywell Road, and its southern edge is Ferry Road, even though some people would argue that Granton proper fades out long before Ferry Road is reached. The northern edge, of course, is the shoreline.

I thought long and hard before I decided to exclude Muirhouse, to the west of Pennywell Road, as in some ways it has a lot in common with West Pilton. I felt, however, that if I included it, I would have been honour-bound to include Silverknowes as far as Silverknowes Road, which is too far west for the purposes of this book. I had no such problem with Wardie, to the east of Granton Road, which has always considered itself part of Trinity. So the book confines itself to the above area, though I have made occasional forays into Wardie and Muirhouse where these have been warranted. In one section, I have even gone as far east as Newhaven.

Granton, over the years, has provided employment for thousands of men and women. This broad expanse of land alongside the Firth of Forth has been home to industry since before the 5th Duke of Buccleuch began building Granton Harbour in 1835. Gas was produced here in what was to become one of the largest gas works in Scotland. Cars, buses and taxicabs were manufactured. A foundry was established. Wire mesh was produced. Railway lines and sidings snaked all over the shore area. Ships left for all parts of the world, and Granton ferries plied back and forth across the grey waters of the Firth, and even got as far as London. It can even lay fair claim to being the birthplace of Scotland's 'Silicon Glen'.

The place was alive with commerce and trade, and though it laid no claims to beauty or elegance, as some parts of Edinburgh did, it more than added to the city's prosperity. By the early 1900s there were over twenty large and thriving enterprises in Granton, and the gas works even had its own railway station, which brought workmen from all over the city to make and supply gas for Edinburgh and Leith.

But Granton's history goes back long before the building of the harbour. Prehistoric man lived in the area, and Romans undoubtedly came this way. There is also linguistic evidence to show that during the Dark Ages (a misnomer if ever there was one), the Angles were here as well. No doubt at that time Granton was within the mighty Anglian kingdom of Northumbria, which, at its height, stretched from the Humber to the Forth.

Granton Castle came much later, as did Royston House, the forerunner of Caroline Park. By this time the area was divided into the two baronies of Easter and Wester Granton, the boundary being the Granton Burn. In the early sixteenth century, Newhaven, to the east of Granton, was established by James IV as a naval dockyard.

In fact, the development of the shoreline shows a gradual move westwards from Leith, as firstly Newhaven and then Granton were established as ports.

So this is the story of Granton, an area which, up until now, has been the 'stranger on the shore' of the book's title. It takes in such unlikely topics as electric cars, the writing of *Annie Laurie*, the Rough Wooing, the Union of Parliaments in 1707, a flying circus – and concrete yachts.

Granton has played its part in the history of Scotland's capital city, and it mustn't be dismissed because it relied for so long on commerce and trade for a living. It has a fascinating history, and was a powerhouse of industry and innovation. I hope that this book sheds some light on this history, and that Granton is a stranger no more.

A plan of Granton 1834 showing only three buildings, the ruined Granton Castle, Caroline House and an estate cottage

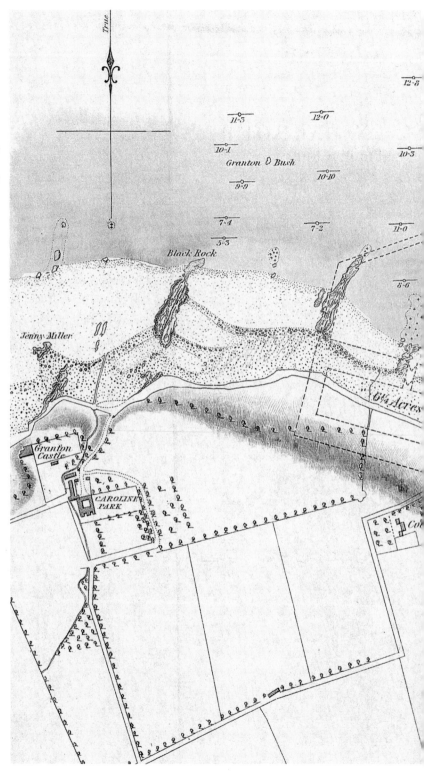

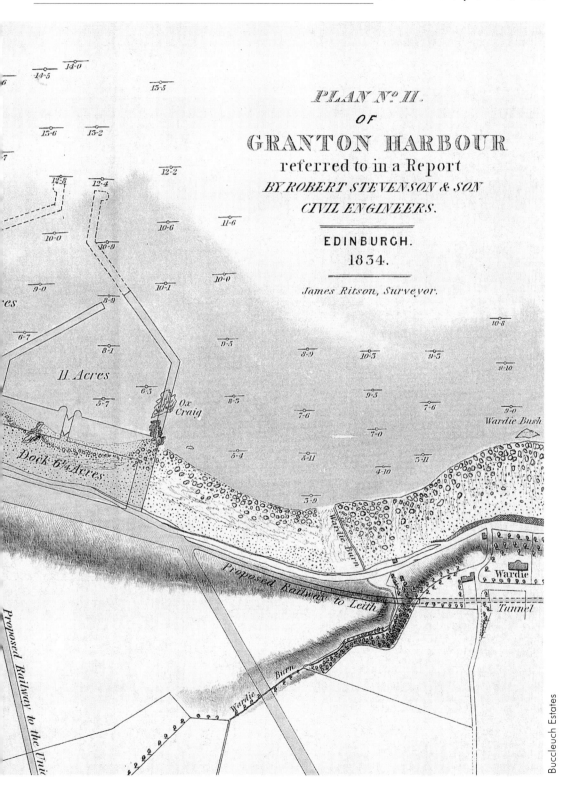

PLAN Nº II.

OF

GRANTON HARBOUR

referred to in a Report

BY ROBERT STEVENSON & SON

CIVIL ENGINEERS.

EDINBURGH.

1834.

James Ritson, Surveyor.

11 Acres

Ox Craig

Dock 6¼ Acres

Wardie Bush

Wardie Burn

Proposed Railway to Leith

Wardie

Tunnel

Proposed Railway to the Uni...

Wardie Burn

The view of Edinburgh from Craigleith Quarry as depicted in a contemporary painting of around 1800. The quarry was much used in the building of Edinburgh's New Town and probably of Granton Harbour. The painting formerly hung in Caroline Park House

Buccleuch Estates

Before 1800

The Early Years

Little or no archaeological evidence remains to tell us much about Granton's prehistory, as subsequent industrial developments simply swept away any trace. A prehistoric stone axe was uncovered close by, and various burial cists have been found along the shoreline, but that is all. Being close to the Forth (an abundant source of food), and having streams (the Granton and Wardie Burns) that could supply fresh water, it was no doubt an attractive spot for early settlers. Here they could hunt, fish and grow crops.

The Romans passed through as well. Cramond, with its Roman fort and port, was only two and a half miles to the west, and Roman pottery was found in 1931 at the site of Granton Castle. It dates from the 2nd century AD, when the Romans were making many incursions into Scotland. It has been suggested that they may have used the Granton shoreline as a landing point. However, no evidence of this has ever been discovered.

By about the 7th century the whole of the Lothians was absorbed into the Anglian kingdom of Northumbria. The very name 'Granton' may come from the Anglian *grand tún*, meaning 'the farm or settlement by the gravel or sand', which no doubt signifies the foreshore of the Firth. Another possible, but less likely, derivation is the Old English *gren*, meaning 'green', and *dun*, meaning 'hill'. Yet again, it may mean exactly what it says – the 'grand', or big 'ton', meaning a town or settlement. But as there was never a large settlement here, this seems unlikely. In the early nineteenth century Crewe Road North was called Whiting Road, a name which has nothing to do with fish. It derives from the Anglian *hwit eng*, and means 'white pasture'. This is not to suggest that hordes of Angles moved north from Northumbria and settled in the area, though some may well have done. But it does suggest that the Anglian influence was strong, and that Anglian was the preferred language.

Scotland emerged as a kingdom in about 843, when Kenneth McAlpin, king of Dálriada (which corresponded to modern day Argyllshire), also ascended the throne of the kingdom of the Picts, and established his capital at Scone. But this fledgling kingdom only took in that area of present day Scotland roughly north of the Rivers Forth and Clyde. There were two further kingdoms to the south – The Lothians and Strathclyde.

The Lothians emerged as a separate kingdom as the power of Northumbria waned. Its capital was at Edinburgh – a name that either derives from–'Edin's town, or fort' (Edin or Edwin being a Northumbrian king) or 'dun eiden', an old British/Welsh name meaning 'the burgh on the hill slope'. It wasn't until about 1018 that Malcolm II took The Lothians into Scotland. Strathclyde was absorbed in 1034 when Duncan, king of Strathclyde, also ascended the throne of Scotland. Thus in the eleventh century Granton found itself within the kingdom of Scotland as we know it today, and the medieval period began.

The Medieval Period

There was never a village or township in the area now known as Granton, so records are slim. Nor was there a Granton parish, as it came within the parish of Cramond, the church of which was two and a half miles away in the village of Cramond. It wasn't until 1877 that Granton got its own parish church.

The Rough Wooing

It was close to Granton Castle (some claim it was where Granton Harbour is now located) that Edward Seymour, Earl of Hertford, landed with an English army in 1544. A contemporary account of the landing tells us that the English fleet had anchored off Inchkeith on May 3, at a spot long called the 'English Road', with the men coming ashore on May 4 at 'Grantainne Cragge'. It was a superbly organised affair, with the whole army disembarking and getting into formation within four hours. It then marched eastwards in three columns, making for Leith, where waiting for them was a Scottish force of five or six thousand men 'in a valley to the right of the said town'. However, it was not one of Scotland's finest hours, as its army – including the commanders – fled the field rather than fight.

There is no mention in this account of an attack on Granton

Castle, though an English force is known to have sacked it at this time. Possibly a contingent of men marched west towards the castle as the main force headed east. It would have made sense to do so, as the castle was the most prominent building in the area at the time.

The English invasion initiated that period known as the 'Rough Wooing'. In July 1543 an agreement had been signed in Greenwich between the Scots and the English that the one year old Mary Stuart, heir to the Scottish throne, would marry four year old Prince Edward, Henry VIII's heir, thus uniting the two kingdoms.

The Scottish Parliament, however, refused to ratify the agreement, and Henry sent troops north to enforce it. Having landed at Granton, Hertford (later created the Duke of Somerset) laid waste to south east Scotland. However, he was defeated at the Battle of Ancrum Moor, and retreated south again. But he was back in February of the following year, laying waste to Melrose Abbey. He didn't follow this up, and waited until the autumn before he invaded again. Finally, in 1547, he won a resounding victory at Pinkie near Musselburgh, though consolidation of the victory proved impossible due to the fact that Edinburgh Castle never fell.

The whole matter was finally resolved in 1548 with the Treaty of Haddington, when it was agreed that Mary should marry Francis, the Dauphin of France and heir to the French throne. She was taken to France in the same year, and the marriage duly took place ten years later. Edward himself eventually married Elizabeth, Francis's sister, and died in 1553, when he had been King of England for only seven years. In 1559 the Dauphin's father, Henry II, died, and for a short time Francis was the king of both Scotland and France (the Treaty of Leith, signed in 1559, recognised both Mary and Francis as 'Sovereigns of Scotland'). If he had lived, and the couple had had heirs, they would have ruled what would in effect have been the United Kingdom of Scotland and France.

The Lands of Pilton

The first recorded mention we have of Pilton dates from 1430, when the lands were owned by the Montgomeries of Eglinton, in Ayrshire. In 1465 David Liddell of Lochtullo held feu over them, and they were returned to the Montgomeries in 1501. The owner by now was Lord John, Master of Montgomery, though he was killed in the

'Cleansing the Causeway' skirmish between the Hamiltons and the Douglases in Edinburgh's High Street in 152 .

The lands then passed through further hands, including that of Peter Rollock, a lawyer who eventually became a judge, assuming the title Lord Pilton. In 1672, by which time they were called Easter and Wester Pilton, they came into the possession of Sir Hugh McCulloch of Cadboll in Ross-shire. In 1688 he died, and now lies buried in Greyfriars Kirkyard.

The next owners were the Ainslies, a Borders family who traded in wine, and had a business in Bordeaux. An inventory of 1657 lists the assets of the lands of Easter and Wester Pilton as being sturdy houses, biggins (old cottages), the manor house of Pilton within its own park surrounded by a stone dyke, walled gardens, outbuildings, a doocot, grain stores and a town house in Stamp Close in the Old Town.

Newhaven and the Great Michael

No history of Granton would be complete without mentioning Newhaven. In the early 1500s James lV, who was later to be killed at the Battle of Flodden, founded a royal dockyard there. He chose Newhaven over Leith due to that port's deficiencies at the time, not the least of which was a great sandbank which barred the mouth of the Water of Leith and prohibited large ships from entering at low tide.

The new port was also known as Our Lady's Port of Grace, and it was here that the largest warship of its time was constructed – the *Great Michael*. The keel was laid in 1507, and every corner of Scotland was pressed into supplying wood or making fittings. Material was also brought in from every maritime country in Europe, almost bankrupting the Scottish treasury. It is said that all the oak woods of Fife – apart from those around Falkland – were cut down and brought to the dockyard.

When it was finished in 1511, it was the pride of the Scottish navy and the envy of both England and France. Over 250 feet long (though some estimates put it at 180 feet) and 56 feet wide, it had sides ten feet thick and four immense masts. It could accommodate 300 mariners (mainly recruited from ports on the Forth) 120 gunners, 1000 men-at-arms, three priests, three surgeons and a musician.

Alas, it saw very little active service. In 1513 it put to sea with the rest of the Scottish fleet under the command of the Earl of Arran (ancestor of the Dukes of Hamilton) and made for France to help that country's navy fight the English. It firstly sailed northwards, which was not so unusual, as heading south would have meant it engaging with the English navy in the Channel. It passed through the Pentland Firth and sailed down the west coast until it reached Ulster. There it bombarded and plundered Carrickfergus, then held by the English. It subsequently put into Ayr to unload its booty, then headed south once more.

Louis of France had expected it to arrive in Brest in August, but it was September before it got there, by which time James IV and the Scottish nobility had fallen at Flodden. By now the fleet was storm-tossed, demoralised, and unfit for combat. So Arran brought the fleet back home, leaving the *Great Michael* and two other ships in the hands of the French. It was eventually sold to them for 40,000 francs, which was a fraction of the building costs.

No one knows what happened to her after that. Some say she lay in the harbour at Brest and rotted away. Others say she was damaged at sea, burnt, or served in the French navy for a number of years. Whatever her fate, she was one of the most remarkable ships ever to have been built in Europe, and she established Newhaven as an important Forth port.

Granton Castle

The first mention of Granton Castle dates from 1479, when it was called Grantoun House. It was owned by John Melville of Carnbree in Fife, and stood immediately to the north west of present day Caroline Park. On his death, it passed to his son, also called John, who was killed at Flodden.

It still belonged to the Melvilles in 1592, when Sir John Melville of Granton sold it to a John Russell. During the next few years it changed hands several times, until, in 1619, it was bought by Sir Thomas Hope of Craighall. However, in 1544, the Earl of Hertford had landed nearby with an English army (*see* The Rough Wooing) and sacked the castle, so his castle must have been rebuilt after this time.

Sir Thomas was Lord Advocate, and the King's Commissioner at the General Assembly which met in Edinburgh in 1643. He made many alterations to the fabric, including a new kitchen wing which projected westwards from the main building, with a wide passage between the two to allow horses to pass from the front drive to the stables.

Granton Castle stood as a ruin from the late eighteenth century

He kept a careful diary of his time there, and in it we read that, on one occasion, he had been unable to sleep one Saturday night due to an attack of colic. However, he rose on Sunday morning and still managed to get to the parish church in Cramond, where he took communion, and was 'greatly comforted' by the minister's sermon.

On his death in 1646, the castle passed to his second son Sir John Hope, his first son having died in 1643. It passed through several hands before finally being acquired by the Duke of Argyll and Greenwich in 1740 when he bought the barony of Wester Granton. The last person to live in it was a Richard Norris, who had married a niece of the second Duchess.

By 1794 it had largely became ruinous, though we know that a gardener at Caroline Park lived in several rooms for a short while in the early 1800s. In 1928 it was bought by a firm of quarriers called Bain and Brown, who demolished it to get at the rock underneath. However, the stratum sloped steeply down into the ground, and the deeper it went, the more uneconomical it became to work. The scheme was therefore abandoned, but not before the natural platform in which the castle stood was lowered by over ten feet.

Today all that remains of Granton Castle is a large fragment of wall, possibly from a chapel, which contains some window mouldings. These

Buccleuch Estates

Caroline Park mansion house which originated in the sixteenth century. John Campbell, the 2nd Duke of Argyll named it after his daughter in 1743. Lady Caroline married Francis, Earl of Dalkeith who was heir to the dukedom of Buccleuch

have been incorporated into the west wall of what was the walled garden, which stood to the east of the castle itself. Also incorporated into the same wall is the castle's doocot. An old photograph shows that at one time it had a chimney, suggesting that it served as a cottage, possibly for one of the gardeners. And next to it are the scant remains of a well.

This walled garden is now a market garden. The present owner's grandfather leased it from the Duke of Buccleuch in 1916, and finally bought it from Bain and Brown in 1928 when the company were still quarrying the castle site. The giant balls which stand atop the piers on either side of the market garden entrance come from the piers of a seventeenth century gateway into the south courtyard of the old castle.

MacGibbon and Ross visited the ruins in the late nineteenth century, and made detailed plans and sketches. They show that the castle was L-shaped, with a turret within the angle of the L, and courtyards to the north and south. An archway led into the north court from the west, and beside it was a 'loupin' on stane', used by horsemen to mount their horses. Above the archway was a panel containing a coat of arms. The main entrance to the castle itself was at first within the turret, though Sir Thomas opened up a grand, new entrance in the south elevation which opened onto the south courtyard.

Caroline Park

By the medieval period, Granton was divided into the baronies of Easter and Wester Granton, with the Granton Burn forming the boundary. The mansion house of Caroline Park was in Easter Granton, and was owned by the Logans of Restalrig. In about 1585 Andrew Logan built a tower house on the site, and most probably this was a square or L-shaped house, as this was the fashion of the time. Whether it was built as a family home, an administrative centre for the barony or what would now be called a 'holiday home' isn't clear. But it would almost certainly have had a bamkin wall surrounding it, and would have had defensive features.

Over the next few years the estate changed hands several times. In 1601 Andrew Logan sold the tower house and barony to Walter Henryson. Then, in 1641 it was sold again, this time to David Johnkin, who sold it on to a man called Partick Nicholl. In 1665 he gave it to his daughter Margaret and son-in-law George Graham of Inchbrace, and in 1676 its name was changed to Royston. The name is supposed to come from the the French word 'roi', meaning king, and the Scots word 'toun'. It was to have been called Kingston, but a nobleman of the time, who already bore that name, objected.

The Gowrie Plot

It was a member of Logan family, Sir Robert Logan, who was implicated in the Gowrie Plot of 1600. James VI, while out hunting, was invited to Gowrie House in Perth by Alexander Ruthven, 3rd son of the 1st Earl of Gowrie and brother of the 3rd Earl, to meet a mysterious stranger who had arrived with a pot of gold. James mistrusted the Ruthvens, as the 1st Earl had held him captive after the Ruthven Raid of 1582, for which he was executed. Not only that – James owed the Ruthvens substantial sums of money.

But greed is supposed to have got the better of the king, and he accepted the invitation. No stranger turned up, and as he was retiring to an upper room after dinner, Alexander and his elder brother berated him for having the 1st Earl of Gowrie executed. Alexander then lunged at the king, saying he would kill him, and James shouted 'treason!' as they fell on the floor together. The king's followers hurried to the scene, and Sir John Ramsay, later to become the Earl of Holderness, killed both Gowrie and his brother.

It is an incident which has fascinated historians over the years. The story about the mysterious stranger with a pot of gold came from James VI himself, and people have treated it with caution. Some have put forward the theory that James, who was known to be bisexual, was enticed to Gowrie when he was promised a night of passion. The fact that Alexander was 20 at the time, and extremely handsome, adds credence to the theory for some.

Sir Robert's involvement in the plot was discovered after his death in 1609, when a letter was discovered in which he admitted hatching the plot with the Ruthvens. Not only that, his stronghold at Fastcastle in Berwickshire was to have been a safe haven for the Ruthvens after the assassination had taken place. Logan's body was exhumed and his grisly remains produced in court, where he was found guilty and later 'executed'.

Viscount Tarbat

Sir George Mackenzie, second baronet of Tarbat, bought the estate in 1683 for £2,111. Born in 1630, he was one of the great statesmen and parliamentarians of his time, and no doubt chose it because of its closeness to the Parliament in Edinburgh while at the same time having a rural outlook. He could also sail from the foreshore to London or his estates in the north. In 1685 he received the title of Viscount Tarbat, and in 1703 was created Earl of Cromarty. It was his grandson, the third Earl, who was condemned to death in London in 1746 along with Lords Balmerino and Kilmarnock for their part in the Jacobite Rebellion. He was later pardoned, though both Balmerino and Kilmarnock were beheaded.

Five years before buying Royston, Sir George had been appointed Lord Justice-General, and was also the chief minister of the king in Scotland. But he was not universally liked, and Claverhouse (Viscount Dundee) once referred to him as a 'great villain'. He was a supporter of the Act of Union, and is said to have sold his vote on the matter for £300.

Though he had bought the house and estate, he reckoned that a simple tower house didn't reflect his influence and importance, so set about enlarging it into an elegant gentleman's residence, though he himself described it as a 'small cottage'. He added a superb south facade in 1696, and it has been suggested that it was designed by Sir William Bruce of Balcaskie and Kinross, who designed Holyrood Palace. If not, then Tarbat himself may have designed it, and was heavily influenced by the architect's style. He also added state apartments which have some of the finest plasterwork in Britain, if not Europe. As well as his other posts, Mackenzie was Keeper of Holyrood Palace, and there is little doubt that the men who worked on the Palace under Bruce also worked on Royston.

In Tarbat's day, the grounds of Royston lay to the south and east of the house, and reached as far south as present day West Granton Road. Two plans dating from about 1740, the year after Tarbat sold the estate, exist. Whether the plans were ever executed isn't known. If they were, then the house had a walled courtyard to the north, with pavilions on either side. Two walls then curved from them towards gate piers and a gate. To the west, running at an angle from the west wall, and following the line of the Granton Burn, was a line of outbuildings, and these may have dated from the time of the original tower house. When the outbuildings were rebuilt after 1740 (with William Adam being the possible architect), the burn had to be carried beneath them via a culvert, which still exists today. Enclosed parkland lay further away from the house, where deer and cattle roamed. This was a typical layout of its period, and showed that its owner had achieved a certain status in society.

But Tarbat seems to have been unhappy with this layout. His interests now lay with Edinburgh, and he no longer spent so much time travelling north to his estates. So he had the south front added, as well as a double-walled court with a gate in the outer wall. A long avenue led southwards from the gate, and another led eastwards. To the east of the house were three rectangular courts, one seemingly filled with trees, one marked 'bowling green' and one marked 'garden'.

Letters between Tarbat and his second son James mention the flowers grown at Royston, and these include daffodils, tulips, anemones and jonquils. The gardener on his northern estates was even asked to send cuttings for hedges. So the house and its immediate surrounding must have been a dignified, colourful and pleasant place.

The Duke of Argyll

In 1714 Tarbat died, and his son inherited the estate. In 1739 he sold it to John Campbell, 2nd Duke of Argyll and 1st Duke of Greenwich for £7,000. Like Tarbat, he was one of the men responsible for the Union of Parliaments in 1707. He had a distinguished military career, and in 1712 was made Commander-in-Chief, Scotland. Always opposed to the Stuart cause, it was his strategies and campaigning which were responsible for crushing the 1715 Jacobite Uprising.

A year after buying Royston, Argyll bought the adjoining estate of Wester Granton, on the other side of the burn, and called the combined estate Caroline Park after his daughter. He was also given the 'right and privilege of a free port or harbour and of founding and building a harbour thereon'. However, he never exercised this right. The purchase included Granton Castle, the barony's main residence.

In 1743, just before his death, Argyll gave the combined estate to his daughter, Lady Caroline, who, a year earlier, had married Francis, Earl of Dalkeith and heir to the dukedom of Buccleuch. Her mother had been maid-of-honour to Caroline of Brandenburg-Anspach, George II's queen, and it was from her that she got the name. Caroline in turn passed her name on to the house and the estate. At the same time Granton Castle was renamed Royston Castle by her father.

The Dukes of Buccleuch

So the estate passed to the Buccleuch family. At the time it was owned by Caroline and her husband, Royston Castle was still in a good state of repair. But in the early eighteenth century the estate was looked upon as a source of income rather than a place of residence for members of the family. Even the oyster beds on the shore were rented out, and brought in an income of £23 a year.

Edinburgh, of course, was by now no longer the powerful seat of government that it once was. The Union of Parliaments in 1707 had seen to that. But an astonishing flowering of scholarship and thought was making it one of the most important cities in Europe. This later became known as the 'Scottish Enlightenment', when men such as Adam Smith and David Hulme promulgated new ideas and new philosophies that had spread throughout Europe.

Though Caroline Park was only a few miles from the teeming centre of the city, it played no great part in it. Unlike the years leading up to the Union of Parliaments, no clandestine meetings took place there, no bargains were struck and none of the great men involved in the movement, as far as it is known, came knocking at its door. It was a quiet, pleasant retreat, surrounded by countryside and with a view out over the Firth of Forth. But it wasn't Caroline and her husband's only home and it became run down.

Sir James Oughton

From about 1767 (some records say 1763) until 1780, when he died, the house was leased to Lieutenant General Sir James Adolphus Oughton, at one time governor of Antigua, and from 1778-1780 Commander-in-Chief of North Britain. When he first took up residence, he wrote that the 'plantings' were entirely neglected, and that cattle were allowed to roam among the gardens. He subsequently repaired the fences and walls at his own expense, and removed some of the features, though what they were isn't known.

In November 1773, he entertained both Boswell and Dr Johnson to dinner at Caroline Park, even though the previous meeting between Sir James and the doctor has almost ended in fisticuffs over the poet Ossian. Boswell gives no account of the dinner, though it must have been a lively affair.

Caroline died in 1793, when the house was occupied by Sir John Stewart of Allanbank, and its ownership passed to her son Henry, the 3rd Duke of Buccleuch.

The Industrial Revolution

The Industrial Revolution was already under way by the late eighteenth century, and many aristocratic families, while not willing to get involved in 'trade', nevertheless saw the new opportunities for income that their vast estates afforded. The Buccleuchs were no different. Ironstone was dug along the shoreline at Granton, and the Cramond parish entry in the first *Statistical Account* (issued between 1791 and 1798) mentions coal as well. Several seams came to the surface above and below the high water mark, and 'when fuel is fcarce', people often came down to the shoreline to collect lumps of coal. The entry also mentions several old coal pits in the 'links of Royftoun', and a pit which was sunk in Pilton in 1788. But the coal was of poor quality, and it was soon abandoned. However, industrialisation was still on a small scale, and contemporary accounts tell us that the main produce of the estate was hay.

So, as the eighteenth century drew to a close, Caroline Park was still basically a country retreat, with the *Statistical Account* calling it 'one of the largest houses in the Lothians'. But industrial exploitation had started, and throughout the nineteenth century, rapid development would take over most of the parkland and gardens, leaving the house marooned in an uncompromising industrial landscape.

After 1800

For the first few years of the nineteenth century there was limited industrial exploitation, and the whole area must still have had a largely rural aspect. But the Scottish Enlightenment was by now over, and Edinburgh was a capital city without a role. Any enterprising Scotsman who wanted to make his way in the world had to look towards London, and the Scottish aristocracy's love affair with that city, which had started when James VI took his court there in 1603, was in full swing. Edinburgh was largely neglected.

But the Industrial Revolution had come to Scotland, offering new paths to money and prestige among the upper middle classes. New technologies opened up new opportunities for wealth. Trade grew quickly. Britain imported cheap raw materials from the Empire, fashioned them into desirable objects, and exported them all over the world. In a few years, it became the greatest industrial nation on earth, and its influence was felt on every continent.

Granton was a microcosm of this. Opportunities for money-making were seized, entrepreneurs moved in and the infrastructures for trade were built. The Buccleuchs, one of the great aristocratic families of Scotland, played the leading role in this when Walter, the 5th Duke, built Granton Harbour in the 1830s, and encouraged rail links to be developed.

A few lone voices – such as that of Lord Cockburn – bemoaned the loss of Granton's largely rural aspect, but most people, including the aristocracy, saw it as progress. The mansion house of Caroline Park was spared, but around it an unashamedly industrial landscape took shape – a landscape that was to define Granton right up until the beginning of the twenty first century.

Buccleuch Estates

Walter Francis, the 5th Duke of Buccleuch, an energetic man with a good grasp of business, built Granton Harbour

The Buccleuch Family

Who exactly are the Dukes of Buccleuchs, who did so much to bring industry and commerce to Granton? They are one of Scotland's oldest families, and with estates in Dumfries and Galloway, the Borders, Midlothian and England, they are one of the country's largest landowners. They originated in the Borders, and trace their ancestry back to Sir Richard Scott, who, in the thirteenth century, married the heiress of Murthockstone, and in doing so acquired her estates. At about the same time, he was appointed ranger of Ettrick Forest, and acquired the lands of Rankilburn as well.

He built his main residence at Buccleuch in Selkirkshire, and from this the later earldom and dukedom got its name. His son Michael fought at the Battle of Halidon Hill in 1333, and was one of the few Scots to escape from what was a rout of a Scots army under Lord Archibald Douglas. However, he was later killed at the Battle of Durham.

By the end of the fifteenth century, the Scotts were one of the most powerful of the Borders families. But like all such families, they constantly quarrelled with their neighbours, especially the Kerrs of Cessford. This came about in 1526 when Sir Walter Scott, laird of Buccleuch, tried to free the young James V from the clutches of the Earl of Angus, who had him 'under his protection' near Melrose. In the ensuing skirmishes Kerr of Cessford was killed, and his kinsfolk got their long-awaited revenge when they killed Sir Walter in Edinburgh in 1552.

Peace finally broke out when Sir Thomas Kerr married Janet Scott, sister of the 10th laird of Buccleuch. Their grandson, Walter Scott (known as 'Bold Buccleuch'), masterminded the famous rescue of William Armstrong ('Kinmont Willie') from Carlisle Castle in 1596.

In 1619 Sir Walter Scott was created Earl of Buccleuch by James VI. His son Francis, however, showed no great loyalty to the Stuarts, and fought against Montrose's troops at the Battle of Philiphaugh in 1645. He died in 1651, aged only 25, and was succeeded by his four year old daughter Mary, who became Countess of Buccleuch in her own right. However, she died when she was 14, and was succeeded by her sister Anna.

Not only was Anna rich and beautiful, she was a young, intelligent woman of great character. This brought her to the attention of Charles II, who sought a marriage between her and his illegitimate son James, Duke of Monmouth. This duly took place in April 1663, with Monmouth being created Duke of Buccleuch. Three years later Anna was created Duchess of Buccleuch in her own right.

In 1685 Monmouth was executed after his rebellion against James VII, and his title forfeited. However, Anna, being duchess in her own right, kept her title, and she lived in Dalkeith Palace until 1732. She is buried in St Nicholas's Church in Dalkeith.

It was in 1767 that Anna's great-great grandson Henry, the 3rd Duke, married Lady Elizabeth Montagu of Boughton, heiress to George, Duke of Montagu. Thus the two houses were united. Then, in 1810, Henry inherited the titles and lands of the Douglases, Dukes of Queensberry, when William the 4th Duke died. Henry's heir was Charles, who became the 4th Duke of Buccleuch and 5th Duke of Queensberry. He was portrayed as 'The Pink Boy' by Sir Joshua Reynolds, and was a close friend of Sir Walter Scott. It was his son Walter Francis, an energetic man with a good grasp of business, who built Granton Harbour.

The present duke (2002) is John, 9th Duke of Buccleuch and 11th Duke of Queensberry KT, and his heir is Richard, Earl of Dalkeith. The present day estates include Queensberry and Drumlanrig Castle in Dumfriesshire, Bowhill, Eskdale, Liddesdale and Branxholm estates in the Borders, Dalkeith in Midlothian, Boughton in Northamptonshire, and properties at Barrow-in-Furness in Cumbria. All are managed by Buccleuch Estates Ltd, which was formed as a company in 1923. It still also owns small parcels of land in Granton.

Caroline Park

Lord Cockburn

From about 1802 until 1835 Caroline Park was leased by Archibald Cockburn, Sheriff of Midlothian, Judge Admiral and Baron of Exchequer. He was the father of Henry Cockburn, better known as Lord Cockburn, advocate, judge and one time Solicitor General for Scotland. As well as being a lawyer, Henry was also a conservationist, and took a great interest in preserving and enhancing all that was best in Edinburgh. The Cockburn Association, also known as the Edinburgh Civic Trust, is named after him. We get a good picture of Caroline Park at the beginning of the nineteenth century from his journals, and alas they are not too flattering about what his father did to the estate. He wrote:

> 'My father did it no good. He was agricultural, and sacrificed all he could to the farm. His friend and landlord – the Duke of Buccleuch – did not prevent him from removing several very architectural walls, a beautiful bowling green, a great deal of good shrubbery, and an outer gravelled court at the north front bounded by the house on the south, two low ornamental walls on the east and west, and a curiously wrought iron gate, flanked by two towers, on the north. Even when he went there, it stood in a wood, quiet and alone. . . The now ruined castle of Royston had still its roof and several floors and windows, and was inhabited by our gardener. The abominations of Granton Pier, with its tram-roads, brickwork, and quarry, had not then been conceived. Winter made little impression on a spot rich in evergreens; the long over-arched alleys were not broken in upon. Every gate had its urns, every bit of wall was dignified by its architectural decoration. The 'Sea-gate', a composition of strong iron filigree work, was the grandest gate in Scotland. The very flowers knew their Goshen[1], and under my mother's care, grew as they grew nowhere else.'

1 The abode of the Israelites during the Plague of Darkness in Egypt

Caroline Park
'Even when my father went there, it stood in a wood, quiet and alone...
the abominations of Granton Pier, with its tram-roads, brickwork, and
quarry, had not then been conceived'

Lord Cockburn
early 1800s

Perhaps it was this destruction that sowed the seeds of conservation in Lord Cockburn's mind. But there is no doubt that his father didn't get his own way everywhere within the estates, as his mother seems to have tended the flower gardens – possibly within the walled garden of Granton Castle – with care.

The description also shows that Caroline Park, at least in the area surrounding the house, had been heavily planted with trees. This is backed up by a description written in 1794 by one John Law, who writes that it wasn't easy to get a clear view of the house because of the trees growing around it.

By the 1800s the Duke of Buccleuch was heavily involved in the industrial development of the area. The truth is that the estate was not, by his standards, a large one. He already owned great swathes of land in the Borders, Dumfriesshire and at Dalkeith to the south of Edinburgh. Caroline Park was small, and probably awkward to manage or exploit in a conventional manner. Industrial development seemed a logical option, with the main development, from the 1800s onwards, being Granton Harbour.

Lady Scott and 'Annie Laurie'

The last member of the Buccleuch family to have lived in Caroline Park was Lord John Scott, one of the Duke's brothers, who didn't quit the property until 1870. Possibly he left when he did because the industrial development going on around the house became too much for a gentleman to bear. By this time Granton Harbour had been built and railway lines snaked through the parkland to the south of the house.

His wife, who was born Lady Alicia Spottiswoode, achieved fame as the woman who gave the song *Annie Laurie* to the world. The first two verses had originally been written by William Douglas of Fingland for Anna (her real name) Laurie, the fourth daughter of Sir Robert Laurie of Maxwelton in Dumfriesshire. She had been born in 1682, and met William at a ball in Edinburgh when she was still a young woman. However, William had a commission in the Royal Scots (which by 1694 he had resigned), and though his own estate of Fingland was only a few miles from Maxwelton, they had never met.

William was struck by her beauty, and a romance blossomed. However, William had Jacobite sympathies, and Anna's father didn't approve. He sent his daughter back to Maxwelton, thinking that would be the end of the matter. But it wasn't. William followed, and soon the couple were meeting on Maxwelton Braes. Anna's father found out, and tradition says that she had to step in when they challenged each other to a duel.

But there was to be no happy ending to the story. William, who was at heart a soldier, heard of a possible Jacobite Uprising, and went to Edinburgh to enlist in the Jacobite army. Later he had to flee for his life to the Continent. In short, Anna had been jilted. In 1702 he eloped with Elizabeth Clark of Glendorth and had two sons, who continued their father's military career. He died about 1760 and was buried at Newland in Peeblesshire.

Maxweltoun Braes are bonnie,
Where early fa's the dew.
And 'twas there that Annie Laurie
gi'ed me her promise true.
Gi'ed me her promise true,
which ne'er forgot will be;
And for bonnie Annie Laurie
I'd lay me doon and dee!

Anna married Alexander Ferguson of Craigdarroch, a relation of William's, when she was 28. It was a happy union, and it appears she gave little thought to William. Her cousin met him many years later, and wrote to Anna about the meeting. 'I trust,' she wrote back coldly, 'that he has forsaken his treasonable opinions, and that he is content. . .' She died on May 5, 1764 at Friar's Carse in Nithsdale, the home of her daughter Jean. Her burial place is unknown, as no headstone has ever been found.

Lady Scott is said to have sat at a clarsach in the Stateroom of Caroline Park as she composed the tune and later set the words of William Douglas to it

The two opening verses of the song first appeared in a ballad book in 1823, and created quite a stir. Who wrote them? Who was this Annie Laurie? Was she a real person? In early 1890 the mystery was cleared up. A letter appeared in the press from a Miss Stuart Monteith, Annie's great grand-daughter, identifying Annie as the daughter of Sir Robert Laurie of Maxwelton, and the writer of the song as William Douglas.

But by this time the song had acquired a third verse, and a further letter appeared, this time in the *Dumfries and Galloway Standard*, from Lady Scott, admitting that she had tinkered with the first two verses and added a third of her own. She also stated that she had set the words to music she had written for an old ballad called *Kempye Kaye*.

Lady Scott is said to have sat at a clarsach (a small Scottish harp) in the Stateroom of Caroline Park as she composed the tune and later set the words to it.

Caroline Park

Ian Moore

Caroline Park is supposed to be haunted by a 'Green Lady', reputed to be the ghost of a previous Lady Royston. Dressed all in green, she rises at midnight from an old well to the north east of the house, goes to a bell pull (now gone) in the courtyard, and rings for admittance to her former home. Whether Lady Scott saw this apparition is not known, but she certainly saw something equally as frightening. She was sitting all alone in the drawing room when one of the windows flew open and a cannonball entered and landed on the floor, bouncing three times. It rolled towards a screen and then rolled backwards and finally settled. Lady Scott called for the servants, but when they reached the room the window had mysteriously closed itself, the glass wasn't broken, and there was no sign of the cannonball anywhere. A Miss Warrander, who was Lady Scott's niece, and who sometimes stayed in the house, often told of strange noises during the night that terrified the servants.

A B Fleming

No aristocratic family would possibly have wanted to live in Caroline Park now that it had a busy industrial harbour on its doorstep and rail lines snaking through its policies. But the Buccleuchs still wanted to earn money from the property, so leased it to AB Fleming & Co Ltd, which owned printing ink works to the west of the house. Here the company set up its main offices, and in 1921 it bought the house outright from the Buccleuchs. It remained as offices right up until 1966, when the company finally moved out. The Duke then bought back the house, and rented parts of it out to families as homes and flats.

Andrew and Birgitta Parnell

On January 6 1988 Andrew and Birgitta Parnell bought Caroline Park and what was left of some of the park and set about restoring it. From 1995 they rented out part of the outbuildings to a firm of magazine publishers, who produced the well-known *Scottish Field* and four marine publications.

The house still belongs to the Parnells today.

Granton House

Another mansion in Granton was Granton House, built in 1807 by the Earl of Hopetoun on land leased from the Duke of Buccleuch. It stood approximately where the Scottish Gas offices now stand, and was a substantial three-storey building with a balustraded roof and 24 rooms.

In 1808 the Earl's daughter had married the Right Honourable Charles Hope, High Court Judge and President of the Court of Session, who sat as Lord Granton. In 1810 a daughter was born, called Margaret, and in later life, as an unmarried aunt, she told many tales of life in the early nineteenth century to her nieces and nephews. They were eventually collected and published as *Tales of a Great Grand Aunt*.

One of the more famous tales concerns a steamer carrying passengers from Stirling to Edinburgh for the State Visit of George IV to Scotland in 1822. Fog came down on the Forth, and the steamer found itself aground on the 'Black Rocks' (though the Birnie Rocks seems more likely) near Granton House. Staff members heard cries for help from the passengers, and Margaret's brother rode to Cramond to see if a rescue boat could be called out.

Meanwhile, her father, knowing that the tide was out, went down to the shoreline and walked across the exposed sand towards the rocks. After some persuasion, the passengers and crew followed him back to the shore, and stayed overnight at Granton House. It was around this time that Sir Walter Scott visited the house on several occasions.

In 1863 the house passed to Sir John McNeil of Colonsay, and it was during the time he stayed there that Florence Nightingale visited. She had come to Edinburgh to advise on the layout of the new Royal Infirmary.

McNeil died in 1883, and the house passed to Lord Gifford, who founded the Gifford Lectures on natural theology at Glasgow, Edinburgh, St Andrews and Aberdeen Universities, and on his death in 1887, it passed to Reginald McLeod of McLeod.

During the early years of the twentieth century, the house was largely neglected. There was a shortage of housing in Edinburgh, and the city council eventually leased the building in 1946 to use as accommodation for homeless families. It, and Restalrig House, which was also leased, cost £2700 each to convert. Granton House took 21 people in 12 families, who were promised they would only be there for two years, though some stayed for much longer. Eventually on the night of January 1 and 2 1954 the house caught fire. Though everyone was rescued, the house itself was badly damaged and was later demolished.

© National Portrait Gallery

When George IV visited Scotland in 1822, he disembarked at Leith bedecked in pink tights, short kilt, and all the supposed accoutrements of a Highland gentleman. The outfit was designed by Sir Walter Scott, who succeeded in making the overweight monarch look ridiculous (as caricatured here by an unknown artist). Fog came down on the Forth on the same day, causing a boat full of dignitaries who had sailed down from Stirling for the occasion to run aground on rocks near Granton House

Arrival of the Royal Yacht 'Royal George' at
Granton Harbour 1 September 1842

Royal Progress – Queen Victoria's early
arrival caused confusion in Edinburgh the
same day

Departure of the 'Trident' from Granton with
Queen Victoria on board, 15 September 1842.
No doubt the Royal arrival and departure
from the new port at Granton was a major
fillip to trade

Buccleuch Estates

Granton Harbour

Even though there was industrial activity of a sort at Granton in the late eighteenth and early nineteenth centuries, it wasn't until Granton Harbour was built in the 1830s that the area surrendered itself completely to industry and commerce. And though Lord Cockburn abhorred it, there is no doubting its success in stimulating trade and making money. The instigator was Walter Francis, the 5th Duke of Buccleuch, and he eventually spent well over half a million pounds on the project, making it one of the largest private building projects undertaken in Britain at the time. A statue of him stands to the west of St Giles Cathedral in the Royal Mile.

The age of the sailing ship was fast being overtaken by steam in the 1830s and Edinburgh was in need of a deep water port.
Walter Francis, the 5th Duke of Buccleuch invested over half a million pounds in the Granton Harbour project, one of the largest private building undertakings at the time

The Beginnings of the Harbour

Edinburgh was desperately in need of a deep water port. The change from sail to steam had increased the number of ships on the Forth, and most had to wait until high tide before sailing into Leith, or relied on small boats coming out from the port to take off passengers and goods when the tide was low. The main ferry between Edinburgh and Fife left from the small harbour at Newhaven, and it meant that there were inevitable delays due to the state of the tide.

In 1833, three schemes were being considered to improve things. The first was the upgrading of Leith, and building a new deep water entrance to the docks from the east. The second was building an entirely new deep water port at Trinity (where there was already a 'chain pier'), and the third was building a harbour at Granton.

The proposer of the third option was Mr RW Hamilton, manager of the General Steam Navigation Company of London. He originally had the idea in 1834, and in February of that year sent a letter to the Marquis of Tweeddale. The Marquis got in touch with the 5th Duke of Buccleuch, who immediately showed great interest. However, the duke was a shrewd man. He knew that there were many powerful people favouring the other options. So he commissioned James Walker, president of the Institution of Civil Engineers, to prepare an impartial report on the three schemes.

Mr Walker duly reported back that the Granton scheme was the best of the three, and the Duke called a meeting of various 'Mercantile and Nautical Gentlemen' at the Waterloo Hotel in Edinburgh under the presidency of Admiral Sir David Milne. He told the assembly that he himself would fund the building of the harbour from his own pocket, and the Granton scheme was approved.

The other schemes still had their supporters, and in 1835 a bill was presented to Parliament seeking permission to build a harbour at Trinity. But it was rejected, and the Duke saw his chance. Work started immediately on a pier at Granton.

But it wasn't until 1836 that the Duke had a bill introduced into parliament seeking permission to build the port as a whole. It stated that great inconvenience, delay and danger was experienced when landing goods and passengers in the Firth of Forth at low tide. It went on to say that the Duke of Buccleuch, at his own expense, had started to build a pier, plus a road linking it to Leith. It also stated that the Duke and his heirs should receive all dues, rates and tolls exacted on the pier and road. However, though there is no doubt the Duke looked on the harbour and the access road as a money-making exercise, he never once collected any tolls on the road. On April 21st 1837 the bill received the royal assent from William IV.

The Central Pier

The first part of the pier was opened on June 28, 1838, which was the day of Queen Victoria's coronation. According to contemporary newspaper reports, there were 'great festivities' at Granton, though the Duke himself was unable to attend, as he was in London for the coronation. But the Duke's brother John was there to inaugurate the undertaking, arriving in his own yacht, the *Lufra*. He named the pier the 'Victoria Jetty' in honour of the young queen.

And it wasn't long before Queen Victoria herself paid a visit. Very early on September 1, 1842 she and her husband Prince Albert stepped ashore at Granton from the royal yacht, *Royal George*. She was received by the Duke of Buccleuch, and set off amid 'the thunder of cannon' for a royal progress through Scotland.

The Queen's early arrival caught most people unawares, and

Edinburgh's magistrates had, on the morning of September 1, 'their slumbers broken or their breakfasts interrupted' so that they could dash to meet her. An elaborate system of signals using guns and flags had been put in place to tell the great and the good of her imminent arrival, but as the morning was grey and misty, the correct signals were not given. In fact, the signal to tell people that the Queen was actually entering Edinburgh was interpreted by some as meaning that her yacht was only entering the Forth.

The Royal Company of Archers, who were meant to accompany the Queen from Granton, eventually managed to meet her coach at Canonmills Bridge. Here they attempted to fall in to the right and left of the carriage, their rightful position. However, a company of dragoons was already there and not knowing that these kenspeckle figures in green were the Queen's official bodyguard in Scotland, the dragoons pushed them back. Fighting and jostling broke out between them, even though the Archers were the elite of the Scottish aristocracy, and Lord Elco, who commanded the Archers, nearly fell under the wheels of the coach. Everything was eventually explained, peace broke out, and the whole procession assumed a more dignified mien.

Meanwhile, the city magistrates and bailies had abandoned their dignity, and were rushing through the town, resplendent in their robes, so that they could intercept the procession near Royal Circus. Most of them arrived just in time to see Queen Victoria pass by, though she gave them no more recognition than the rest of the crowds lining the route.

On the return journey to London, the Queen and Prince Albert sailed south from Granton, this time aboard the General Steam Navigation Company's vessel *Trident*, which was the fastest in their fleet. It was specially decorated for the occasion, and made London in record time. In fact by the time the Farne Islands were reached, it had out-distanced all the accompanying ships in the flotilla.

The pier, however, still wasn't finished. It now had to be continued out into deep water, and the Duke's workmen made use of a diving bell so that work could go on beneath the water line. By October 1844 the 1700 feet long pier was complete. It had, contemporary accounts tell us, ten berths for large steamers, some of which could be over 1,000 tons.

On September 5 of the same year, a new pier on the Fife side of the Forth at Burntisland, had opened. The building of it had been a partnership between the Duke of Buccleuch and Sir John Gladstone, a Liverpool merchant who traded with India. Two years previously an act of parliament had allowed both Sir John and the Duke to transfer the Fife-Edinburgh ferry which ran from Pettycur to Newhaven to a new route between Burntisland and Granton. The route was therefore shortened by two miles, and the ferries could run no matter the state of the tides. The journey took between '80 to 45 minutes' depending on the weather.

The Breakwaters

But a pier was not enough. There had to be breakwaters to enclose it and keep heavy seas from the dock areas. It was decided to build two – one to the west and one to the east. This would not only protect the port, it would offer future berthing facilities and increase Granton's handling capacity. A further act of parliament was granted royal assent in 1842, and work got underway on building the western breakwater, which was to jut out in a north easterly direction before turning almost due east. By 1849 the first 1,500 feet section was complete. A couple of years later and it had been extended to 3,100 feet, which is nearly three fifths of a mile.

The eastern breakwater was started in 1853. Curiously, the outer 1,000 feet was built first. The stone was brought from Granton Quarry along the western breakwater then taken by a wooden bridge across to this new section. The remaining section was then built out from the shore line and the two were joined. When finished, it was 2,100 feet long, and led due north from the shoreline before turning north west towards the tip of the western breakwater. It was wider than the western breakwater, being 25 feet wide at the top and 150 feet wide at its base.

Thus the two breakwaters enclosed a large area of water, leaving a narrow entrance between the two extremities where ships could enter. Running up between the breakwaters was the original pier, creating a West Harbour and an East Harbour. Of the two, the west one was the bigger, with an area of 69 acres at high tide, while the East harbour had an area of 52 acres.

It was a simple but effective layout, and soon it wasn't just being used as a port, but as a place of refuge for ships of all nationalities caught in storms on the Firth. The Duke encouraged this, and charged only a penny per ton as a toll, as it brought the new port to the attention of many ship owners and merchants throughout

Europe. In fact, he laid down many mooring buoys so that the ships could stay within harbour without taking up berthing space. For ships of the Royal Navy he charged nothing at all.

The West Pier

The Lothian coalfields were now expanding rapidly, and this, coupled with an increase in trade, meant that Granton needed further facilities. The Duke of Buccleuch therefore decided to convert the inside portion of the western breakwater into a commercial quay.

The cost was enormous, and again the Duke met it from his own pocket. A protection wall was built on the seaward side, and a road and two rail lines laid along the top of the breakwater. Timber wharves, one 800 feet long, were constructed, and in 1860 two steam driven cranes were erected to handle coal. Set in masonry foundations, each could raise 20 tons at a time. The facilities were the most modern in Scotland for handling coal, and in a day they could load 700 tons. As late as 1927, one of the cranes was still working – and working well. When the project was finished, 2,000 feet of deep water berthage was available, and it had some of the most modern facilities of any port in Scotland.

The Beginning of the Twentieth Century

At the start of the twentieth century, Granton was a thriving port. Throughout all this, however, it lay outside the boundaries of Edinburgh. All this changed in 1900. On 30th July an act of parliament was given its royal assent which brought the harbour within the boundaries of the city. Two years previously the city had bought 110 acres of land west of Granton Harbour, on what had been the barony of Wester Granton, to build a gas works that would serve both the city and Leith. The site was chosen largely because of the dock facilities, and in 1902 coke from the works began to be exported to Scandinavia.

However, ships were getting larger, and dredging had to be carried out to accommodate the increased draught. The next fourteen years were ones of prosperity. The port didn't have to rely on the tides, and because of this imports were at a high level, and coal and coke exports doubled.

TRADE FIGURES—YEAR 1936

	VESSELS		GOODS			
	No. of Arrivals	Net Regd. Tonn.	Imports — Tons	Exports — Tons	Fish landed Tons	TOTALS — Tons
Petrol Imports . .	12	21,276	31,782	...	...	31,782
Asphalt do. . .	3	5,481	3,489	...	...	3,489
Esparto do. . .	60	91,658	79,964	...	...	79,964
Wood Pulp Imports .	26	8,899	10,749	...	...	10,749
Strawboards do. .	28	1,890	2,754	...	...	2,754
Sundry do. .	8	1,677	4,302	...	...	4,302
Coal and Coke Exports .	331	174,473	...	603,157	...	603,157
Sundry Exports . .	2	698	...	1,029	...	1,029
Trawlers, etc. . .	3,027	264,660	...	...	10,784	10,784
Sundry Lighters, etc. .	296	20,643	...	...	...	...
	3,793	591,355	133,040	604,186	10,784	748,010

The trade figures for the year of 1938 at Granton harbour

Buccleuch Estates

World War I

This prosperity brought Granton to the attention of the Admiralty, and at the outbreak of World War I the Middle Pier was requisitioned. Trawlers from fishing fleets based all over the Forth were berthed there, stripped of their fishing gear and converted into minesweepers. Gradually other parts of the port were requisitioned also, and by the end of the war only one third of the West Pier was used for commercial purposes. By 1918, the navy flotilla consisted of 58 minesweeper trawlers, 57 escort trawlers, 8 drifters, 25 motor launches, 6 paddle sweepers, 1 whaler, 6 yachts and 29 special service vessels, all armed. The special service vessels were Q-ships with hidden guns which tried to lure U-boats within range before dropping their disguise. On March 31 1920 the Admiralty handed the port back to its management.

Two 25 ton steam cranes had been installed between 1912 and 1914, and ancillary works put in place to take their great weight. Additional areas were also needed to take coal wagons, and it was decided to reclaim land from the sea along the shoreline of the Western Harbour. A retaining bulwark was built linking the shore

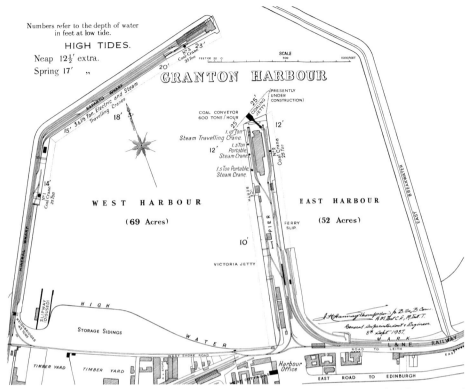

A plan of Granton Harbour in its heyday at the time of its centenary in 1937. The plan bears the signature of JH Hannay-Thompson, Chief Engineer and Superindent of Granton Harbour Ltd

ends of the middle pier and western breakwater, and behind it the area was infilled. By 1917 the infill was complete, with new rail lines snaking everywhere.

Up until 1932 the Harbour had been run and owned by the Buccleuch Estates. But that year a major change came about. A private limited company was formed, of which the 7th Duke was chairman. It didn't alter the management of the port to any great extent, and it continued to run profitably and efficiently.

In 1937 the building of a new coal jetty got under way. 1937 was also the centenary of the harbour, and the Duke of Buccleuch laid a commemoration stone on the Middle Pier. It has since been removed, and can now be seen at 4 Granton Square.

World War II

There were 14 serious air raids on Edinburgh during the war, and one of them was on Granton Harbour. On the night of July 23 1940, starting just after midnight, an aircraft dropped over 100 incendiary bombs, most of which missed their mark.

A number of people were injured in the raid. One woman was

The deep water coaling berth operating in the 1930s. (top and bottom) The 25 ton coaling cranes, of which Granton Harbour had three, could each ship 300 tons of coal every hour

overcome by fumes as she watched from her window, and a mother and baby were taken to hospital suffering from shock. One bomb even landed in a front garden, then bounced into a bedroom, where it lay, still fizzing, while the occupants got out. And at 5.45pm on September 29 a German bomber returning from an aborted raid on Rosyth dropped a 500lb bomb on a block of flats at 21-27 Crewe Place. Number 27, on the ground floor, was occupied by Sandy and Peggy MacArthur and their two children, Ronald and Moira. Peggy was thrown into the back garden by the blast, but was relatively unhurt. However, her two children were still inside the building. The rescue services toiled for over two hours, and discovered that Ronald had taken the full force of the blast, and had been killed outright. Moira was still alive, though on her way to hospital she too died.

Also killed was Charles Wilson, who lived in number 25, above the MacArthurs. Seven other people were seriously injured, and 23 slightly injured. The block of flats was subsequently repaired, though

A tanker discharging oil at Granton in the 1930s

it was given a flat roof instead of a sloping one. It can still be seen today.

Towards the latter part of World War II, a small shipyard with a slipway operated at the head of the east breakwater. James Morton & Sons built eleven 45 foot motor fishing vessels here.

After the War

An ammunition dump was opened just after the war in a yard behind Caroline Park, which was patrolled by soldiers with fixed bayonets. However, there was a certain laxness in their vigilance, and some Pilton people still remember, as children, stealing items from it such as guns and cordite fuses. At one point police found them playing at cowboys and Indians with, of all things, Berettas which had mother-of-pearl handles. And on another occasion two boys stole half-inch diameter cordite, and took it to an Anderson shelter in Granton Crescent, where they ignited it. They were both injured in the subsequent blast.

During the war the harbour had been requisitioned by the Admiralty, and it was not until 1946 that commercial work got under way again. For a few years the levels of trade enjoyed in the pre-war years was maintained, though there was an irreversible slump in coal exports as the Lothian fields were being worked out. But this also meant that there was not enough coal for the adjoining gas works, so imports from North East England rose.

One incident still remembered by the older people of Granton is the bombing of the 38,000 ton HMS *Nelson* in the River Forth in 1948 and 1949. She was anchored to the west of Inchkeith, and planes of the Fleet Air Arm from Donibristle in Fife and the RAF at Turnhouse used her for target practice, though the bombs weren't armed. However, if any of the bombs ricocheted off HMS *Nelson* and landed in the water, a great plume went up which could be seen for miles around. The best view could be had from the top deck of a number 19 bus at Granton Square, and many people used to clamber aboard just to see how the target practice was going.

Later the ship was taken to Wards of Inverkeithing to be broken up – a sad end to a ship which had been launched in 1927, and on board which the Italians surrendered to the allies off Malta in September 1943.

Things got back to normal after the war, and once again the port thrived. A second-hand floating dry dock was acquired, and came into operation in 1947 when the trawler *Coadjutor* entered it to be overhauled. And in 1953 a transit shed was constructed on the Middle Pier.

The harbour employed many local people, and at this time played a prominent part in Granton's New Year celebrations. No one in the area watched the clock for the approach of midnight on December 31, or waited for the 'bells'. Instead they listened out for the boats in the harbour. Every one of them, at the stroke of midnight, blew their hooters and horns in unison, a joyous racket which could be heard all over the north of the city. Only then would people wish each other a Happy New Year and open the Ne'erday bottle. This not only celebrated the New Year, it also heralded a yearly seven day's holiday for the fishing fleet.

A new oil discharge terminal was completed on the West Pier for the Regent Oil Company in 1961, with the first tanker to discharge being the *Texaco Oslo* of 18,810 tons. And in 1967 a roll-on/roll-off berth for heavy indivisible loads was built on the Middle Pier.

The present Duke of Buccleuch, who was a director of the port from 1947 until 1968, remembers the *esprit de corps* of the harbour staff. There was, he says, a pride in the harbour. An annual staff party even took place in an upper room of the Granton Tavern.

The Duke of Buccleuch was the licensee of this establishment, and his name was above the door. One of the great mysteries of the pub was why the yearly profit was always £20 either side of £400. Eventually it was let out for a larger yearly rent.

There were also many characters worked at the Harbour. One in particular was a crane driver, who always delighted Middle Eastern crew members by addressing them in Arabic, which he had learned while a soldier in Egypt.

When the post-war Labour government wanted to nationalise all docks and harbours, it was met with fierce opposition from the workforce, led by the foreman, Walter Beveridge. He was not only chairman of the Transport and General Workers Union in Scotland, he was also a first cousin of Jenny Lee, Aneurin Bevin's wife. Nothing more was heard of the threat for another twenty years.

Granton Harbour in the 1960s was still a busy port, though not perhaps as busy as it once had been. In 1961 it was decided to reclaim 25 acres of land from the Western Harbour by infilling, and this duly took place over the next ten years. A new industrial estate was created, one of the first developments being the Len Lothian warehouse. When it was built, it was the largest warehouse of its kind in Scotland, with 140,000 square feet of space.

In the mid 60s, the Rochdale Report was published, recommending the grouping of ports in various British estuaries under a single authority. A bill was presented to Parliament, and in January 1968 a new body called the Forth Ports Authority took over the management of most of the ports on the Forth.

The nationalisation of Granton Harbour was a decision which pleased those who were in charge at Leith. They had always been jealous of Granton, which was one of only two ports in Britain making a profit at the time (the other being Felixstowe). When nationalised it employed 86 people, and by 1970 this had been reduced to two. The dredger *Rockchime* was also sold off, and the harbour began to silt up.

It eventually closed as a commercial port in 1974, and a year later the last Northern Lighthouse Board's tender, stationed at Granton for the last hundred years, moved its berth to Leith. Nowadays activity is mainly confined to the East Harbour. And as sail once gave way to steam, so the harbour has given way to sail once more. It is now given over to yachts belonging to both the Royal Forth Yacht Club and the Forth Corinthian Yacht Club.

Darney Devlin

Thomas Leishman Devlin
owner of the largest trawling
fleet to sail from Granton

The Fishing Fleet

One other industry thrived at Granton Harbour, and that was fishing. The trawling fleet amounted to about 80 vessels at its height between the wars, each one working the North Sea fishing grounds.

In 1885 the first steam trawlers started working out of Granton. It was the ideal port for them, with deep water at all times. It was also ideally placed to fish the North Sea grounds and supply Central Scotland, all of which was within a day's journey of the port. The first trawlers were small, and usually managed three trips a week to the fishing grounds, which were close to the coast. But as larger vessels were introduced, so they trawled the whole of the North Sea.

The largest trawling fleet was owned by T L Devlin, founded by Thomas Leishman Devlin. His father, also T L Devlin, had been a herring buyer, but young Thomas wanted to broaden his business base. Unable to secure a stance at the Newhaven Fish Market, probably due to religious prejudice (he was a Catholic), the story goes that he came out of the market, stood on a couple of fish boxes, and there and then started auctioning fish on commission from the foreign trawlers which were unloading. They too were discriminated against in Newhaven at the time, so they were more than willing to sell to him.

Using the money he earned, he then set about building up a fishing fleet, which eventually became the largest private fleet of steam trawlers in Britain. He did so by purchasing second-hand steam trawlers, and eventually placing orders for new ones with James Robb, shipbuilders in Leith.

Needless to say, he acquired a stance at Newhaven Market. A story is told of him always walking the full length of the market to get a drink of water, though he had a tap in his stance office. People used to wonder why he did this, until a fish merchant overheard him saying to an assistant when he got back from such a walk, 'Don't sell the sole until I tell you'. The fish merchant then realised that Thomas had a photographic memory, and was scanning and remembering the range of fish his competitors had on offer.

Between the wars was the heyday of Granton fishing fleet. Trains left every day taking fish to markets. This view shows the Middle Pier from Granton Square

Devlin's was one of the few trawling companies that had its own yard. Here it did repairs to its fleet, and, unusually for a trawling company, made its own timber fish boxes. During both World Wars it supplied backup to the Royal Navy, as there were many trades employed there, from carpenters to coppersmiths and electricians. It was during the two World Wars that many of the trawlers were converted to mine sweepers.

Devlin's also had a net factory employing mainly women and retired trawlermen. Women made the new nets, and the retired trawlermen repaired them and dipped them into a deep tar well at the rear of the premises before hanging them up to dry.

The heyday of Granton as a fishing port was between the two World Wars. Fish trains left every day, taking fish to markets in Glasgow and the North of England, and the industry supported many smaller companies around the harbour area.

Devlin's was not the only trawler firm working out of Granton. There were others, such as Croan's, Boyle's, Carnie's and Paton's. A number of them grew out of Devlin's, as they were founded by men who once skippered a Devlin trawler. Paton's was a Glasgow company with a presence in Granton, and their trawlers all had names ending in 'Paton'. Devlin's, boats, however, mostly had names taken from Latin, and staring with the letter 'C'.

The trawlermen were not well treated by some of the companies. If one of them was badly injured at work, for instance, then he was finished. On one occasion, a crew member was on deck in the dark, and stumbled. Firstly his trousers, and then his leg, got caught up the trawl wire. He was pulled along the deck towards the sheave (a grooved wheel fitted into a steel frame to support the wire). His leg was too big to go through, so it was pulled clean off. He had to leave the fishing industry without one penny of compensation.

In December 1939, at the outbreak of World War II, German planes were active above the North Sea, and the Granton trawler *Compagnus* was attacked, when 150 miles east of the Isle of May. One member of the crew was killed and another seriously injured. On the following day another trawler, the *Isabella Grieg*, was also attacked, though the crew survived. Then, on the 19th, a third Granton trawler, the *River Earn*, was attacked and sunk. All were rescued.

After World War II the fishing industry started up again. Half a million hundredweight of white fish was landed each year to begin with, and to achieve this, the boats now had to travel great distances, and be away for ten to twelve days. In 1949 a new fish quay was opened in the Middle Pier, but by then catches were dwindling, the fleets were greatly reduced in number, and lorries took the place of fish trains. Devlin's disposed of their last four trawlers in the early 1960s.

In late 1949 the fleet suffered its only natural loss, when the 276 ton *Margaret Paton* went down with all hands on a trip to Norwegian waters. She had set sail from Granton on December 18 with a crew of 13, heading for her normal fishing grounds in the North Sea. During a radio message received on December 22 the skipper, Mr Stevenson (a Portobello man), said that all was well, and that they would be home in time for Hogmanay. She was never heard from again. No one knows what happened. On December 29 a fish box with the Paton logo and a *Margaret Paton* life belt was washed ashore south of Stavanger in Norway.

After the New Year holidays, the trawler owners wanted their crews to return to sea, but they refused, saying that they wouldn't go back as long as there was a hope that the *Margaret Paton* crew members were safe. On January 6 the RAF called off its search for the missing vessel, and the crews then agreed to return to sea after a memorial service had been held.

This duly took place in St Andrew's Church in Newhaven, conducted by the Rev Duncan H Neilson, and attended by the Lord Provost of Edinburgh, Sir Andrew Murray. Hundreds wanted to attend, but most were disappointed, as the church was too small. The church doors were therefore left open so that those outside could at least hear the hymns. A collection raised £108 7s 5d, and this was

The steam ship Daily Chronicle which became the Commadator, one of the TL Devlin Ltd fleet

Motor Trawler Granton Merlin which was operated by Croan Trawlers Ltd and then by British United Trawlers Ltd, Granton

Buccleuch Estates

donated to a fund that had been set up for the dependents of the lost men. Hibernian Football Club donated £250, and by the end of five days there was over £500 in the fund. By the time it closed, nearly £3,000 had been raised. Most Granton people knew the men who had drowned, and the whole community was badly affected by the tragedy.

1956 saw the arrival of the Granton's first diesel trawler, and soon over 20 were sailing from the port. But by now now it was obvious that Granton's fishing industry wasn't prospering, due to over-fishing of the North Sea and fierce competition from abroad. In the early 1960s Associated Fisheries, which had bought up various local fishing fleets, pulled out altogether, and in 1978 the last trawler sailed from Granton.

One surprising thing about Granton harbour was that, even though it supported a busy port, fish could be found in it, which shows how clean the water was.

Esparto Grass

After World War II, Granton accounted for a third of the 200,000 tons of esparto grass imported into Britain annually. It came from North Africa and Southern Spain, and was used in paper making. At that time there were twenty paper mills being supplied, eleven of them within the Lothians.

Up until 1861 paper was made almost exclusively from rags. But in that year the duty levied on paper was abolished, and the industry could expand and look for new raw materials. There was an increased demand for quality paper, and rags couldn't meet the demand. Esparto was the answer.

Nowadays wood pulp is the chief raw material used in making paper, but high quality papers still demand a rag and esparto content. Weight for weight, paper with an esparto content is 20 per cent thicker than paper made from wood pulp alone.

Granton's association with esparto grass brought an unexpected bonus for the children of the area, in the form of tortoises. Some of these animals would be found hiding among the grass in the holds by dock workers.

Oil and Petroleum

The first oil and petroleum company to set up at Granton was the Anglo-Saxon Petroleum Company, which built huge oil storage tanks close to the West Pier in 1909. By the mid fifties there were six bunkering points on the West Pier and tankage on the Middle Pier .

Granton never imported crude oil for the refinery at Grangemouth. This mostly came from the Finnart Ocean Terminal on the banks of Loch Long by pipeline. Instead it handled refined oil only, importing it by large tanker and then distributing it by small coastal tankers and a fleet of tanker lorries to a number of places in the UK. It also serviced the needs of the shipping which used the port, including the trawler fleet. Storage space for 20,000 gallons was erected close to the Middle Pier for this. Granton's Shell installations also handled domestic fuels, gas oil, kerosenes, and bitumen.

The Regent Oil Company built a new terminal at Granton in the 1960s costing over half a million pounds. It stood opposite the West Pier, across the railway lines from Anglo Saxon, and could store eight million gallons. The West Pier itself could take tankers of up to 18,000 tons, being discharged through 10 and 12 inch diameter 'docklines' at up to 2000 gallons a minute.

Ferries

Granton in its early years became the principal passenger port on the south side of the Forth, with daily sailings to Fife, Dundee, Montrose, Aberdeen and the Moray Firth.

It is sometimes stated that the world's first roll-on/roll-off rail ferry was introduced at Granton, running between the harbour and Burntisland in Fife, but this is untrue. This honour belongs to Northumberland, where the Bedlington Coal Company ran one which took wagons filled with coal from Blythe Harbour to Shields Harbour at the mouth of the Tyne and began operating in 1842.

Nor were engines or coaches routinely taken across the Forth on a roll-on/roll-off passenger ferry. Train passengers alighted at Granton Harbour and took a ferry to Burntisland, where they got onto another connecting train.

There were six ferries – the *Express*, the *Granton*, the *Burntisland*, the *Forth*, the *Auld Reekie* and the *Thane of Fife*. In 1878 the *Express* was withdrawn as her boilers had worn out, and she was replaced by the *John Stirling*, which was much bigger. She was replaced by the *William Muir* in 1879.

This was possibly Granton's most famous ferry. It was named

Two of the ferries that plied betwen Burntisland and Granton, The Willie Muir and the Thane of Fife. This photo is from March 3 1937 when the Thane was taking over from the aging Willie Muir. The William Muir was built by J. Key and Co. of Pettycur and was arguably the most well-known vessel in all the years of the Granton-Burntisland crossing.

On December 28 1879 the William Muir carried the 75 passengers who, when they embarked on their connecting train in Fife, would be killed in the Tay Bridge disaster after a director of the North British Railway Company, and was given different names according to where you lived. If you came from the New Town, it was the William Muir. If you lived in Trinity, it was the Willie Muir, and if you lived in Pilton it was the Wullie Muir. She later gave her name to a pub (now gone) which stood to the north of West Granton Road.

She was built by J. Key and Co. of Pettycur, weighed 412 tons gross and was 174 feet long, with a beam of 24 feet and a draught of ten feet. Her steam engines were built and installed by Ramage and Ferguson of Leith. She sailed right up until March 3 1937, when the *Thane of Fife* took over. But on March 20 1940 all ferry operations on the Forth ceased due to the War, and the *Thane of Fife* was commandeered by the Admiralty. She spent the war plying between Granton and Port Edgar at South Queensferry.

The most famous ferry crossing was made by the *William Muir* on December 28 1879. This sailing carried the 75 passengers who would be killed in the Tay Bridge disaster. The party of officials who headed for Dundee from Edinburgh when news of the disaster broke made the crossing on the *Leviathon*, but as passengers only. There was no train aboard, and contemporary accounts tell us they had to wait for over an hour at Burntisland for a train to take them on to Dundee.

However, Granton can lay claim to having the world's first roll-on/roll-off ferry that operated via public rail tracks, when one started operating in 1850. The Bedlington operation was on private tracks, and once the wagons reached their destination, they never continued their journey by train. The Granton ferry was introduced to take, not carriages, but wagons aboard four 'goods boats' – the *Leviathon* (the most famous one), the *Robert Napier*, the *Balbirnie* (the largest) and the *Carrier*. All were designed to operate on the Tay as well, as were some of the six ferries. The only instance of a laden passenger train being taken onto a goods boat (the *Robert Napier*) was on the Tay, in 1851, at the inauguration of the ferry service there.

At first it was thought that the wagons could be lifted by cradles attached to cranes and put aboard the ferry, then lifted out at Burntisland by the same method. This proved impractical, and a simpler method was devised. Rail lines already ran to the head of the Middle Pier. A set of movable lines, which could be extended or retracted according to the state of the tide, was connected from the fixed rails on the pier to a set of rails already fitted on the ferry

The William Muir at Granton

deck, which could take up to 30 wagons. A stationary steam engine drew four wagons at a time up onto the pier, or lowered them onto the boat. It is ironic to think that the man who designed this arrangement was the same man who designed the bridge that collapsed – Sir Thomas Bouch. The goods boats continued in service until the Forth Rail Bridge was opened in early 1890.

But Granton passenger boats didn't just ply across back and forth to Fife. In 1871 the General Steam Navigation Company ran a service from Granton to Irongate Wharf in London, using three vessels – the *Stork*, *Heron* and *Ostrich*. There were two sailings a week, on Wednesday and Saturday, both leaving at 3pm. They arrived in London on Friday and Monday mornings respectively.

Just after World War II, a proposal was made by Forth Ferries Ltd. to reintroduce a ferry using four former tank landing craft, and the Ministry of Transport gave permission in March 1949. The company's managing director was Sir Andrew H Murray, then the Lord Provost of Edinburgh. The landing craft were sent to Lamont's

MV Glenfinnan in service in the early 1950s

Shipyard in Glasgow for modifications, especially on the bow section, which had originally been designed for beach landings.

It had been intended that the ferries would run as soon as the modifications had been carried out, but it wasn't until July 1950 that the L.T.C 4-673-50 arrived at Granton and was renamed *Bonnie Prince Charlie*. She was 180 feet long, with a beam of 34 feet, a draught of 7 feet and could do 12 knots. She was joined a few days later by another craft (L.C.T. 4-893) which was renamed *Flora MacDonald*. Finally the *Eriskay* and the *Glenfinnan* joind them. All had been built in 1943, but at various yards.

The first summer season was a great success, and the vessels were joined by two ex-Admiralty launches, the *Forth Lady* and the and *Ulster Lady*, which offered pleasure cruises from Granton and Burntisland to the Bass Rock and the Isle of May.

But after that initial season it never prospered, and soon the company was in debt to the tune of £250,000. It couldn't pay its harbour dues, and solicitors therefore initiated centuries old procedures which involved nailing warrants to one of the ships' masts (the *Flora MacDonald*). Alas, when the solicitor's clerk turned up with the regulation hammer and nails, he was flummoxed to find that the masts (such as they were) were made of metal. In those days before sticky tape, there was little he could do about it. The ferries stopped running on July 12 1952, and the company was wound up in September 1953. The vessels were eventually sold to an Indian shipping company.

Between 1991 and 1993 a catamaran called the *Spirit of Fife* ran between Granton and Burntisland, with a free bus service to and from Edinburgh city centre. However, by this time the Forth Road Bridge had been opened for over twenty five years, and it never prospered.

HMS Claverhouse

The Royal Naval Artillery Volunteers was formed in the 1870s, when it looked as if there would be a war between Britain and Russia. For a few years the organisation prospered, but then went into gradual decline through official neglect.

When it eventually folded, the Admiralty realised just how important it had been, and in 1903 formed the Royal Naval Volunteer Reserve (RNVR) in its place, the first divisions being on the Thames, the Clyde and the Mersey. It was an immediate success, attracting a large proportion of yachtsmen to its ranks. These men already knew about the sea and boats, and the London division even had a company entirely made up of men who worked on the Stock Exchange.

HMS *Claverhouse*, the Forth Division of the Royal Naval Reserve, was founded in 1913, when a unit of the Clyde Division was formed in Leith. By World War I it had eight officers and 100 men, and in 1922 obtained its own ship, moored in Leith Docks, which it converted and named HMS *Claverhouse*.

The division grew in strength all through the 1920s and 30s, and by the outbreak of war in 1939 it had 433 officers and ratings, and of those 35 were killed on active service.

In 1949 the division acquired a minesweeper, which it named HMS *Killiecrankie* and from then on HMS *Claverhouse* specialised in training volunteer reservists for minesweeper duties. HMS *Claverhouse* eventually moved to Granton, and was moored alongside the Middle Pier. The present Duke of Buccleuch served on the vessel, and when she was scrapped, he suggested the Granton Hotel building – which by now had ceased to be a hotel, and had been used for a time to accommodate displaced persons – as a temporary base.

In 1995 HMS *Claverhouse* moved out, and the following year it was taken over by the Territorial Army. It remained unoccupied until early 1998, and from that date it has housed a field hospital, Royal Marine Reserves, a detachment of the Royal Naval Reserves, an Army Cadet Force and a unit of the Sea Cadet Force.

The Yacht Clubs

There are two yacht clubs in Granton – the Royal Forth Yacht Club and the Forth Corinthian Yacht Club. The former was founded for gentlemen yacht owners who hired professional crews to race them, while the latter was one of a number of Corinthian clubs encouraged by the government to provide a pool of officers for the Royal Navy.

In December 1835, 36 gentlemen met at the Royal Hotel in Edinburgh and formed the Eastern Regatta Club, which, with William IV's permission, changed its name in the following year to the Royal Eastern Yacht Club. Its object was to organise an annual yacht regatta on the Forth, and the first one duly took place off the Leith Roads in 1836. Further regattas took place in the 1840s, 1859 and the 1860s.

However, it was felt that an annual regatta was not enough, and on May 16 1868 a new club, the Granton Sailing Club, was formed. Four years later it changed its name to the Forth Yacht Club, and in 1881 moved to a clubhouse on Boswall Road. In 1883 it changed its name yet again to the Royal Forth Yacht Club.

A further yacht club was founded at Granton in 1897, and this was the Almond Yacht Club. In 1957 it merged with the Royal Forth, and in 1959 the first Heligoland Race (now held every two years) was organised. In 1969 the Royal Eastern merged with the Royal Forth as well, creating the club it is known it today.

In 1984 a new clubhouse was opened on the Middle Pier. The club has run various Scottish, British, European and world championships in its time, and now has a membership of over 500.

The Forth Corinthian Yacht Club's history is not so convoluted. It was founded in 1880 in the Granton Hotel and the Wardie Hotel on Lower Granton Road. Fifteen years later it moved to central Edinburgh, occupying three different addresses over the next 73 years – South St Andrew Street, Blenheim Place and Royal Terrace. In 1968, however, it returned to its roots, and established itself at 1 Granton Square, formerly the harbour master's house and office.

Private yachts have used the Eastern harbour at Granton since the middle of the nineteenth century. Individual moorings were originally laid by yacht yards from Leith, but after World War II this was done by the Royal Forth and the Forth Corinthian clubs themselves. Forth Ports dredged an area next to the Middle Pier in the mid 1990s, and the clubs paid for and installed pontoons. The Royal Forth and the Forth Corinthian are now equal partners in the Edinburgh Marina Company, which manages the pontoons for the benefit of club members and visiting boats, which come from all around the North Sea.

The two clubs work closely together to improve facilities at Granton for recreational and racing sailors, and indeed collaborate with the other clubs on the Forth under the auspices of the Forth Yacht Clubs Association. The waters off Granton are ideal for yacht racing, and there is a regular programme of races throughout the sailing season. East Coast Sailing Week, a major yachting event, comes to Granton every three years and attracts boats from the Tay to the Tyne.

Courtesy of Royal Forth Yacht Club

Liz Tulloch

A painting of the Royal Forth Regatta at Granton 25 July 1859

(below) The Regatta in the Forth in modern times

Goods wagons shunting
beside Newhaven Road

Empty coal wagons leaving
Granton Harbour. Granton
was connected to the national
rail network from 1879. This
lasted until the 1980s

The Railways

If it hadn't been for the railways Granton Harbour would never have been the success it was. In some ways, it was the first deep water port specially built in Scotland to take advantage of rail links, thanks to the foresight of the Duke of Buccleuch. Fifteen years after Edinburgh's first ever railway line opened, Granton had its own rail link.

Edinburgh's first line ran for eight and a half miles to Dalkeith. It had a double track, a gauge of 4 feet 6 inches, and was used to bring coal from the Lothian coalfields into the heart of Edinburgh. The first part of the line was opened in 1831, and ran between a goods yard at St Leonards, close to the Salisbury Crags, and a colliery at Craighall. The following year it was extended to Dalhousie Mains near Dalkeith. The wagons were pulled by horses, except for a short stretch at St Leonards where a steam-driven winch pulled them up a steep incline. At a later date, a branch line was opened from Niddrie Junction which headed north west towards Portobello and on to a station at South Leith.

Edinburgh, Leith and Newhaven Railway

Not long after, in 1836, an Act of Parliament for the Edinburgh, Leith and Newhaven Railway received the royal assent. It was to start at Canal Street Station, near the present Waverley Station, and run north through a tunnel beneath the New Town, emerging at Scotland Street, where there was also to be a station. From there it was to go to the main entrance of Leith Docks. A second line was to branch off at Heriot Hill, cross the Water of Leith, and make for Newhaven, where it would once again divide, one branch going towards a station at the Chain Pier and the other going to Newhaven Pier.

The cost was to be £100,000, though this was greatly increased when the rail company found itself embroiled in litigation with householders in the New Town who objected to a tunnel which might affect the foundations of their homes. Other land owners also objected, and the course of the rail line had to be altered at various places.

In 1840 it was decided to approach the Duke of Buccleuch about extending the line to Granton Harbour. The Duke, not unnaturally, was delighted with the idea, and in 1844 an Act of Parliament was obtained to carry out the work. A line would branch west from the main line just before the original Trinity Station, and head towards the harbour (a new Trinity Station was later built, and the original one became a goods yard). At the same time, the idea of a line towards Leith (with a station at Bonnington) was resurrected, and this too was given the go-ahead.

In 1847 the whole line from Canal Street to Granton was finally opened, the journey taking all of 15 minutes (even though the trains were hauled through the tunnel by winch towards Scotland Street). A timetable was introduced which allowed for a train every half hour, with extra trains for early morning ferry departures.

By this time the name of the company had been changed to the Edinburgh, Leith and Granton Railway, and it proved a great success. In the same year the Edinburgh and Glasgow Railway began extending its line east from its terminus at Haymarket to a new station at North Bridge, and this enhanced the Granton line ever further, as people could travel from Glasgow, change at North Bridge, and continue on to Granton by way of Canal Street.

However, the line beneath the New Town didn't last long, and in 1868 passenger services were withdrawn, with a new line from Piershill to Trinity taking its place. In 1887 the down track was removed, the space being used for growing mushrooms and the up track used for storing manure wagons. In 1847 the Edinburgh, Leith and Granton Railway was bought by the Edinburgh and Northern Railway, which became the Edinburgh, Perth and Dundee railway in 1847. It in turn was bought by the North British Railway in 1862, and it continued to run passenger services from Waverley to Granton, which were finally withdrawn in 1925.

In the 1890s, during the construction of Waverley Station, Canal Street Station was demolished and the entrance to the tunnel destroyed. However, most of the tunnel still runs beneath the New Town, and in 1980, when the Waverley Centre was being built, it was rediscovered. A plaque in Waverley Station now records where the tunnel started.

Caledonian Railway

But Granton wasn't just served by the Edinburgh, Leith and Granton Railway. In 1846 a bill was presented to Parliament by the Caledonian Railway for the building of a line from Slateford to the harbour, but this was rejected. A year later, however, the company was given permission to build a link between Slateford and Haymarket, at that time the Edinburgh terminus for the Edinburgh and Glasgow line. Then, in 1857, a joint bid by the Caledonian Railway and the Duke of Buccleuch to build a line between Granton and the main line south to Carstairs was successful.

Work began in 1858, and in 1861 it opened for freight. It approached the harbour from the south west, passing through the former estate of Caroline Park, and ended in a fork, one line going towards the Western Breakwater and one to the goods and mineral depot and on to the Middle Pier, and at the same time joining up with the Edinburgh, Leith and Granton Railway. Stations at Murrayfield and Craigleith were served by a passenger service from Princes Street to Leith which started up in 1879, and which also stopped at Granton Road and Newhaven.

Thus Granton Harbour was connected to the national rail network. Two branches eventually came off the Caledonian line, one heading west to Barnton from Craigleith Junction, with stations at House o' Hill and Davidson's Mains, and one heading eastwards from Crewe Junction towards Leith, with stations at East Pilton, Granton Road, Newhaven and Leith North. In addition, a line left at Newhaven Junction, and headed for a goods yard at Leith, with intended passenger stations at Ferry Road and Leith Walk that were never opened. The Caledonian Railway had wanted to take this line round to Lochend and back to Princes Street Station through a tunnel, giving Edinburgh a northern suburban loop, but permission for it was denied.

In 1902 a spur was laid which ran off the Caledonian line and into the gas works. This brought coal and other goods to the gas works, and a station was built so that workmen could board a train at Princes Street Station and travel straight to their place of employment. Further dedicated spurs for freight only were also built – one to AB Fleming's printing inks works and one to Robert Mushet's ironworks.

A short line called the Mineral Line (also known as the 'Duke's Line') was also laid between the gas works and the harbour for bringing in coal and taking out coke and tar. A 'tally man', employed by the Duke, stood day and night in a small shed close to the present Caroline Park Avenue, making a note of what came in and out so that the Duke could make a charge for each wagon.

The rail lines continued to serve North Edinburgh and Granton Harbour for many years. However, in 1942 Granton gas works station shut down. Then, in the wake of the government's Beeching Report, the line itself between Crewe Junction and Granton was closed in 1965. There were still sidings at the harbour however, connected to a line from the old Leith North Station. When these closed in the early 1980s, Granton lost its final link with the rail network.

The Pilrig tram makes its way through Newhaven en route to Granton, c. 1910

Robert Grieves collection

The Trams

In the early nineteenth century, there was no local public transport in Edinburgh. Short distance stage coaches ran to places like Leith, Corstorphine and Portobello, though these were outwith the city, and separated from it by green fields. By 1830 omnibuses – pulled by horses – were running between Edinburgh, Leith and Newhaven. But this was as near as they got to Granton, which at that time was still a rural area.

Trams came to the city on Monday November 6 1871, when the Edinburgh Street Tramways Company opened a line between Bernard Street in Leith and Haymarket, with the trams again being pulled by horses. The fare from Haymarket to Register House was 1d outside and 2d inside, and the fare for the whole journey was 2d outside and 3d inside.

And though the Edinburgh Street Tramways Company opened an omnibus service between Newhaven and Granton in September 1882, it wasn't until 1909 that tram lines eventually reached Granton.

Trams connected Granton to the rest of the city between 1909 and 1956 when they were finally withdrawn in favour of buses. Under new plans drawn up by the Waterfront project, trams will once again run to Granton from the city centre, stopping at intermediate points

A twin-tracked extension of the Leith to Newhaven line was built, which would take the trams as far as Granton Square, where they would turn up into Granton Road and continue along it and thus onto Ferry Road.

Granton Road marked the boundary between Edinburgh and Leith at the time, with the boundary running down the middle of the road. Each track would therefore be in a separate burgh, causing problems when it came to planning and rating issues. They were eventually solved by giving ownership of the tracks to Leith.

The Granton trams were powered by electricity, as were most of the trams in Leith. In Edinburgh, however, most of the trams were powered by a cumbersome, continuously moving cable just beneath the surface of the street. A system of grippers on the underside of the tram gripped the cable and pulled it along. If it wanted to stop, the grippers were released and the brakes applied.

To make the system more reliable and cost effective, it was decided to electrify all the lines. In 1922 the first electric tram service, no 123, ran up Leith Walk and easily crossed over onto what had originally been a cable track at the corner of Pilrig Street, the former city boundary, and continued on its way to Nether Liberton. However, a party of university students, aggrieved that they hadn't been invited to the official launch, boarded it and either hung from the sides or sat on the roof – a dangerous thing to do – until it reached its destination.

But by the early 1950s motorised buses were perceived to be the new way forward, and a proposal was made to abandon the tram system completely. There was much opposition to this, but eventually Edinburgh City Council agreed. Lines began to be lifted, starting with those on Ferry Road to the west of Granton Road, which had been laid for a proposed Crewe Toll extension that was never used. The first service to be withdrawn was Waverley/Comely Bank, in 1952.

The first Granton tram to be withdrawn was Granton Square to Newington Station via Broughton Street (service no 8). This took place on April 8 1955. It was closely followed by the 'Granton Circle' and Churchill trams (service numbers 13 and 14) in June. By September 1956 there were only two tram services operating in the city – Morningside Station to Granton Road Station (service no 23) and Braids to Stanley Road (service no 28), both running via the Mound.

The final day of Edinburgh's tram service was Friday November

16, 1956. The Granton Road Station service ran until nearly 7.30pm, though buses had already taken over the route earlier in the evening. After a ceremony on the Mound, three trams and a horse bus made their way along Princes Street, and turned off for St Andrew Square. The horse bus then made its own way to the Shrubhill depot in Leith Walk. The trams continued along York Place and down Leith Walk. They paused at the Shrubhill gates, watched by thousands, and passed through into the depot, with the gates closing behind them. By 9.40pm the electricity that had powered the trams for all those years was turned off, and the Edinburgh tram system was no more.

Granton History Group

This photo from the mid-1950s shows Tram Service No 9 outside HMS Claverhouse ready to head up Granton Road to Goldenacre, Broughton and Colinton. The tram at the rear is Service No 8 still on the 'out' rails. The Trolley Boom needs to be swivelled round (by the conductor) before the No 8 can get on the 'in' rails and head up Granton Road to Goldenacre, Broughton Road and Newington Square

© Ken Barry Photography

Granton's heritage as an
industrial hub from the early
nineteenth century is evident
from this modern view from
Leith westwards

Industries

G ranton's heritage from the early nineteenth century onwards has been almost wholly industrial. Since the building of the harbour, it has been defined by that commercial, money-making vigour first displayed by the 5th Duke of Buccleuch. It was one of the first areas close to Edinburgh to embrace wholeheartedly the new technologies that were coming to the fore during and after the Industrial Revolution, and because of this it contributed to the city's continuing prosperity.

And over the succeeding years it continued to do so. A roll call of the companies which traded in the area contains many names. All offered employment to people from all over the city and their names should be recorded and applauded.

Granton Quarry

Quarrying had taken place along the foreshore at Granton for many years before 1835. But in that year the biggest quarry of them all was opened by the Duke of Buccleuch at Granton Point, right on the shoreline. It was to become the second largest quarry in the Edinburgh area (only Craigleith was bigger), and its stone was used in building Granton Harbour. It was a clear indication that the Duke had, by this time, decided to concentrate on the industrial exploitation of his Granton estate.

It cut deep into the sandstone rock, so much so that it covered eight acres and its bottom was 80 feet below sea level. It employed between 50 and 60 men, some of whom lived in what were known as the 'Quarriers' Cottages' on the West Shore Road, which stood until the early 1970s. Even after the harbour was complete, it still continued to operate, and the statue of Nelson atop Nelson's column in Trafalgar Square was made from the stone quarried here.

The entrance to the quarry was down a sloping plane, with a stationary engine at the top to haul up wagons of stone. Around it

Granton Quarry made the pages of the London Illustrated Times in 1855 when the sea wall embankment collapsed, Stone from the quarry had made the Nelson statue at the top of Nelson's Column in Trafalgar Square

was a broad road, and at the west end was a house where Robert Muir, the overseer, lived with his family. In the basement of the house was a steam engine connected to a powerful pump drawing up water from the bottom of the workings. Robert was a keen gardener, and according to contemporary accounts, he cultivated the top of the embankment between the quarry and the sea, growing, among other things, early potatoes.

The quarry had one other claim to fame, and that was a great fossil tree which had been uncovered during excavations. Both geologists and members of the public regularly made their way there to see it. Newspaper accounts call it an *Araucaria*, and it was 75 feet long and tapered from five to two feet in diameter.

During the autumn of 1855, the quarriers had been following a fine stratum of sandstone, which was heading northwards, at the west end of the quarry. As they worked they became anxious that the wall between the quarry and the sea might be breached, but the Duke ignored their warnings. So concerned were the men, however, that they downed tools, and the Duke moved them to the south face of the quarry to allay their fears.

In October there were some violent storms, with prolonged westerly gales and high tides. The quarriers expected the worst, but by Thursday 25 the gales dropped to a gentle breeze and they heaved a sigh of relief.

The storms, however, had already done their damage. At between 3am and 4am Robert Muir was wakened by a curious noise unlike anything he had heard before. It wasn't the pumps, which were still pumping away in the basement of his house, and it was only when he saw a great crack in his bedroom ceiling, which was widening before his eyes, that he knew what was happening. The embankment was giving way, and house was falling into the sea.

Quickly he wakened everyone, and called down to the boy who attended the pumps, telling them to leave immediately. As they were doing so, half the house fell into the quarry as the embankment finally collapsed. The waters cascaded in, flooding the workings within five or ten minutes. Had it happened after 6am, when the workmen clocked on, there would have been a large loss of life.

Thousands of pounds worth of equipment lay at the bottom of the quarry, and in 1856 diving bells were used in an attempt to salvage it, but to no avail. A news story in the *Illustrated Times* of November 10 1855 states that the quarry would therefore not reopen. An accompanying sketch shows a desolate scene, with the quarry flooded and an old building – possibly the overseer's house – perched precariously on the edge.

For several years the quarry lay abandoned, used occasionally as a bathing place by locals and as a harbour for oyster boats. Then, in 1884, it became the headquarters for Scotland's first marine station. And for some time it acted as a winter berth for the pleasure steamers of the Galloway Steam Packet Company of Leith.

Granton Gasworks

Twenty six years after William Murdoch – a Scotsman – first used coal gas to light his house and offices in Redruth in Cornwall, gas lighting came to Edinburgh. In 1818 the Edinburgh Gas Light Company began distributing gas from its works in New Street, off the Canongate.

Then, in 1823, the Edinburgh and Leith Gas Light Company started up in opposition, siting its works at Baltic Street in Leith. A third company joined the fray the following year – the Edinburgh Oil Gas Company. It had its works at Tanfield, and its chairman was Sir Walter Scott, who was so enamoured of gas lighting that he had it installed at Abbotsford. This company didn't last long, and was absorbed into the Edinburgh Gas Light Company in 1829.

The two remaining companies competed for several years, each one laying its own separate gas mains, sometimes in the same street. It was a costly business, and in 1866 they agreed to divide up the area between them. But in 1888 both Edinburgh City Council and Leith Town Council decided that it would be more cost effective if there was one overall gas production plant for both towns, and this resulted in the formation of the Gas Commission for Edinburgh and Leith. It was a wise move, because between 1890 and 1900 Britain's gas consumption experienced a 42 per cent increase. Sites at Craigentinny and Granton were looked at for the building of the new gas production plant, and eventually Granton was chosen, because of the harbour and its rail links.

In 1898 the commissioners purchased 106.5 acres of what had been the Wester Granton estate from the Duke of Buccleuch for £124,000. This gave the commissioners plenty of scope to expand if need be, and kept the works away from densely populated areas. A bill was presented before parliament for the building of the gas works, and it received the Royal Assent on May 23 1898.

The foundation stone was laid in October 1899 by Mrs Mitchell Thomson, wife of the Lord Provost of Edinburgh. A handsome plaque was incorporated into one of the buildings to commemorate the event, and a casket containing various documents sunk into concrete below the foundation stone. The engineer responsible for the design of the gas works was Walter Ralph Herring, and his initial plans (which still exist) vary greatly from what was actually built. They show eight gas holders instead of the one that eventually materialised, seven retort houses and a 'deep sea harbour' on the shoreline where the flooded Granton Quarry once stood.

The first part of the plant was completed in 1902, and in the same year gas production was started. In February 1903 it was formally opened, the ceremony being a grand affair, with many speeches and an orchestra placed atop the gas holder. The whole thing was illuminated by gas jets mounted on the cast iron thistles and roses which adorned the outer lattice work on the holder, and which were four feet high. By 1905 the rest of the works had been completed, the total cost being £842,000, including the purchase of the land.

In 1920 Leith became part of the city of Edinburgh, and in the same year the Gas Commission for Edinburgh and Leith was dissolved. The running of the plant now became the responsibility of Edinburgh City Council, which formed a gas committee with a convener, vice convener and fourteen council members.

By 1926, when a new vertical retort plant was inaugurated by the Duke and Duchess of York (later to become George VI and Queen Elizabeth), over 200,000 tons of coal was being used each year to produce just under three billion cubic feet of gas. As by-products,

120,900 tons of coke was produced, 12,900 tons of tar and 2450 tons of sulphate of ammonia. The coke was sold as a smokeless fuel, the tar went to road building and chemical manufacture, and the sulphate of ammonia was used as a fertiliser.

The plant had over 114,00 consumers, and served an area that covered Joppa in the east to Balerno in the west through 483 miles of mains, some of them 4 feet in diameter. In addition, there were 1500 miles of piping carrying the gas from the mains to the consumers. There were over 900 workers, and the annual wage bill was £148,000.

In 1928 a second gas holder was erected to take the increased production, and the plant remained more or less like this until the time of World War II. The works were never bombed, even though German bombers flew up the Forth. The joke was that this was because number 2 holder had been bought from a German company called Mann, and Hitler had ordered it to be spared as it hadn't yet been fully paid for.

After the war the gas works were nationalised, along with most of the other gas undertakings in Britain. In 1949, they were at the centre of a most unusual controversy. It could be summed up thus – what is the most suitable colour for a number 2 gas holder? The manager of the works, Mr DD Melvin, considered the matter to be of the utmost importance, and at a meeting of the Edinburgh Council Planning Committee said that grey was the most suitable colour, with sky blue as an alternative. However, the Council's Chief Planning Officer, Mr D K Plumstead, disagreed, and said that golden yellow was best. The arguments put forward for grey were that this shade of graphite paint would be more resistant to corrosion, would camouflage the holders in the event of another war, and would cost only £9,000, whereas golden yellow would cost an extra £5,000.

To counter this, Mr Plumstead said that a warm and cheerful colour such as golden yellow would harmonise with the 'varying backgrounds seen from many different viewpoints' and would have better reflective properties which would diminish the outline of the holder. He further said that it was impossible to camouflage such large objects unless they are put underground or covered in camouflage netting. A no doubt bemused Planning Committee decided that it wasn't competent enough to resolve the issue, and asked the opinion of the Royal Fine Arts Commission. In the end, the holder was painted blue.

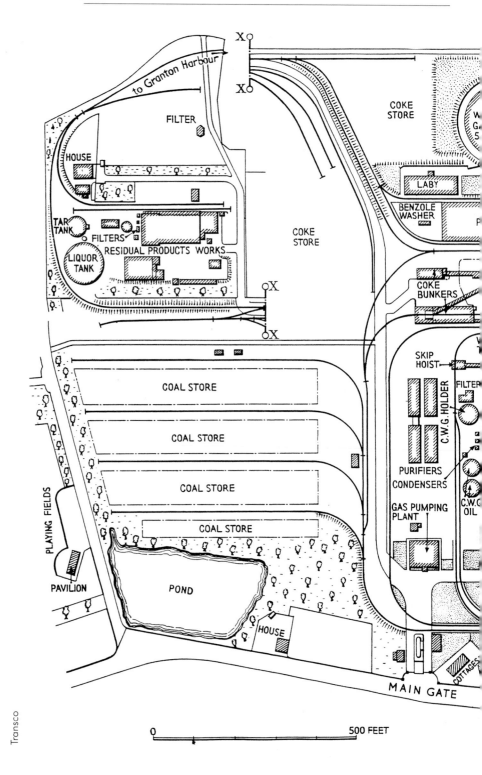

to Granton Harbour

X
X

FILTER

COKE
STORE

W
G
S

HOUSE

LABY

BENZOLE
WASHER

TAR
TANK

FILTERS

COKE
STORE

RESIDUAL PRODUCTS WORKS

LIQUOR
TANK

COKE
BUNKERS

X

X

SKIP
HOIST

COAL STORE

FILTER

C.W.G. HOLDER

COAL STORE

COAL STORE

PURIFIERS
CONDENSERS

C.W.G
OIL

GAS PUMPING
PLANT

COAL STORE

PLAYING FIELDS

POND

PAVILION

HOUSE

COTTAGES

MAIN GATE

0   500 FEET

Transco

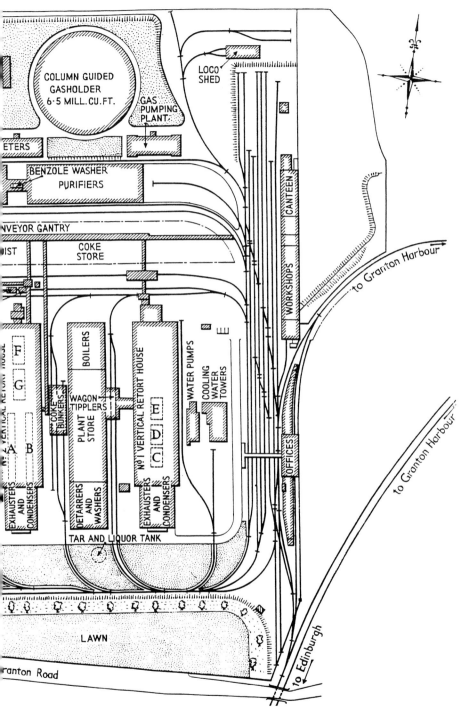

A plan of the Granton gasworks which at one time employed 900 people and produced 12 per cent of Scotland's gas as well as coke, tar and ferliiser

No improvements were made to the gas works until 1962, when equipment for what is called the Onia-Gega self steaming process was commissioned. This took crude gas, a by-product of oil refining, and reformed it into town gas. It involved laying a 16 inch diameter main from Grangemouth to Granton and the building of two Humphreys and Glasgow reforming plants on site. A further 12 inch diameter main was laid from Granton to Falkirk and Armadale so that the resultant gas could be fed into the distribution system. The total cost of the scheme was £1.36 million, and it was completed in 1963. Further improvements to the gas works took place in 1966 and 1967, including the building of a third holder.

One unusual feature of the gas works was a flooded quarry (which is still there) to the south of the site, hard against West Granton Road. The water from this was used to cool various pieces of equipment, and it was fed by a pipeline from the flooded Craigleith Quarry, which at one time was the biggest and deepest quarry in Edinburgh. One of the most famous features of this quarry, before it was flooded, was a fossilised shark uncovered by the quarriers. Craigleith was later filled in, shark and all, and the site has now been built over.

By the late 1960s natural gas from the North Sea was coming on stream, and Granton gas works had to adapt. In 1970 a new 18 inch diameter pipeline was laid from Broxburn to Granton, bringing natural gas to the plant. Edinburgh was the last part of Scotland to be converted to natural gas, so from 1970 until 1976 Granton took the North Sea gas and turned it into town gas.

In 1986 the gas industry was de-nationalised, and in 1987 Granton closed down as a gas production plant. By 1992 the works had been de-manned, and it became instead a storage and distribution facility controlled firstly from on site and then from a central control in Newcastle.

At its height, the Granton gas works was one of the biggest producers of gas in Scotland. In the early 1960s, just before natural gas became the preferred option, it was producing 35million cubic feet a day, and this was increased by a further 18million cubic feet in 1963 using the Onia-Gega self steaming process, an amount which alone accounted for one eighth of the gas used in Scotland.

As part of the redevelopment of the Edinburgh Waterfront, new offices for Scottish Gas will be built on the former gasworks site, which is also the planned location for a new Telford College campus.

Madelvic Motors

The Madelvic Motor Carriage Company was founded with a capital of £25,000 in January 1898 by William (later Sir William) Peck, the Edinburgh City Astronomer. Within a year a factory at Granton had been built at a cost of £33,000, complete with a test track. It was reputed to be the first purpose-built car factory in Britain, with a handsome office block of red brick edged with stone.

Madelvic 'electric brougham' built at William Peck's Granton factory 1898. Note the fifth wheel which powered the vehicle. William Peck's idea was ingenious but not a commercial success

The production units where the carriages were actually assembled were, as one observer said, 'completely right for car production', and they still stand today. One has two storeys, with steel floor supports and uncluttered working areas, while the adjoining area is single storey with a glazed roof.

Peck is described by those who knew him as being 'charged with an infectious enthusiasm but of the voluble sort'. He was born in Castle Douglas in 1862, and as well as being an astronomer was a prolific inventor. He patented various devices to do with internal combustion, as well as pumps, propellers, optical instruments and ignition devices for cars. He also wrote books, such as the *Handbook of Astronomy*, and the *Observer's Atlas of the Heavens* and *Constellations and How to Find Them*.

He may well have been an inventive man, but he sadly

A Kingsburgh

Robert Grieves

About 1902 the Madelvic factory was occupied by John Stirling who built lorries and buses. This picture shows Stirling lorries at Joppa, passing what today is the Rockville House Hotel

An example of a Stirling bus built at Granton and supplied to a company in Orkney where this view was taken at Kirkwall

misinterpreted the needs of the public when it came to motor cars. Firstly, he saw electricity as being the way ahead, and secondly he looked on the motor car as being a substitute for the horse and carriage. His own vehicle was driven by a 'fifth wheel' located behind and between the two front wheels, and carried the carriage along at a pace which was no faster than a horse. So proud was Peck of this arrangement that he had a carving of the wheel incorporated into the balcony above the main entrance to the offices. But he also hedged his bets, as shafts were incorporated into the carriage so that a horse could take over if the electric motor failed. A contemporary of Peck was taken on a trip in one of the carriages, with Peck driving, and he describes how the great man would occasionally stop the carriage, dismount, and retrieve an object that had fallen off.

In February, one month after the company was founded, Peck had secured a contract from the Post Office to carry mail between Leith and Edinburgh. But this failed to impress the general public,

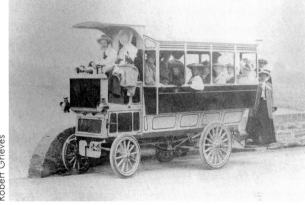

Robert Grieves

Stirling's Motor Carriages Ltd achieved success with their buses and this batch was exported to Western Austrlia. They are pictured here in Perth

who even then expected a motor car to be faster than a docile horse. By April 1900 the company was in trouble, and sought a further £25,000 from the banks to continue trading. The banks, however, had had enough, and the company folded.

The Kingsburgh Motor Company bought it for £13,000, and built a number of small motor cars on the site. But soon it too was in financial trouble, and in 1902 it was bought by Stirling Motor Carriages, based in Hamilton. Its main products were buses and lorries rather than cars, and it bought in most of the components.

In about 1905, The Scottish Motor Engineering Company was formed by a man called Glingoe. He was backed by several wealthy men, and began building buses and bus chassis. These were fitted with a 40hp four cylinder engine, with speed being regulated by a centrifugal governor which controlled the cylinders. The greater the speed, or the heavier the load on the engine, the more cylinders came into play. It was a novel system, but it never caught on, and in 1908 the company closed down, to be replaced by Granton Engineering.

In 1912 it too folded, and Peck re-emerged with a scheme to build taxi-cabs, and founded the Caledonian Engineering Works. He took several hundred orders from taxi owners and firms in London, but couldn't raise the capital to finance the building of the vehicles themselves.

During World War I the factory was used for storing torpedoes, and was finally bought by United Wire in 1925. Today the core of the original factory still exists, more or less as it was when vehicles were manufactured there.

Northern Lighthouse Board

The Northern Lighthouse Board was created by an Act of Parliament in 1786. Four lighthouses were then built, at Kinnaird Head near Fraserburgh, North Ronaldsay on Orkney, Eilean Glas at Scalpay and the Mull of Kintyre. However, the first lighthouse in Scotland was built privately on the Isle of May in 1635. It consisted of a stone structure on top of which coal burned in a brazier. Nowadays there are over 200 lighthouses looked after by the Northern Lighthouse Board, stretching from Muckle Flugga in Shetland to Chicken Rock off the Isle of Man.

From 1802 until 1852 the Board's main store was in Leith, but in that year it took a five year lease on a site in Granton from the Duke of Buccleuch for £110. Here it relocated its stores in what is now West Harbour Road, and from 1874, also moored *Pharos*, the lighthouse supply tender, in Granton harbour. It subsequently renewed the lease, and between 1868 and 1869 built the red-brick store and buoy shed that still stands today.

In 1874 the experimental light tower was added. Though it looks like a lighthouse, it never served as one. Instead lighting and optical equipment was tested there before being taken out to be used on the main lighthouses. In 1892, long before the vast complex of the Granton gas works was built further to the west, the area's first gas works was built on the NLB site.

Granton was the ideal site for the stores, and in 1907 they were improved and extended, with a railway siding and a travelling crane being added. But by the 1930s, acetylene was taking the place of coal gas, and the gas works closed down and were removed.

Pharos was the flagship of the Northern Lighthouse Board, and in 1955 the predecessor to the present vessel moved permanently to Leith. But the stores still had a role to play, and in 1969 another buoy store and a plant store was built behind the existing buildings. Even in 1990, by which time *Pharos* had been decommissioned and there was no NLB tender stationed on the Forth, the stores were being extended.

But in 1996/97 the depot closed down completely, and part of the site was returned to the Buccleuch Estates. The engineering storage and test facility still remained until November 2001 when it moved to a modern site at Oban ending the Northern Lighthouse Board presence in Granton.

United Wire

In 1798 a Frenchman called Louis Robert first thought of using a continuous form of wire cloth for manufacturing paper. The paper's raw materials – wood pulp, esparto grass, flax, or other vegetable fibres – were first beaten up with water to produce a wet mass of loose cellulose fibres which were then laid on the wire cloth. The water drained through the wire, leaving a thin layer of fibres which, when dried, became paper.

The process was later introduced into Britain by Henry Fourdrinier, and together with an engineer named Bryan Donkin, had a machine up and running at Frogmore in Berkshire in 1803.

Twenty two years later, in 1825, William McMurray set himself up as a 'wire worker' in Glasgow's Trongate, manufacturing such items as fire guards, mouse traps and bell pulls. Twelve years later he moved his company, now called the 'Edina Wire Works' to Steads Place, off Leith Walk in Leith, and took on his step-brother James as a partner. There is no reason to suppose that he moved to the Edinburgh area because the city was Britain's leading centre for printing and paper manufacture. Nevertheless, it was to prove a smart move, as the business prospered.

A finished Machine Wire made by United Wire Works at the old Madelvic factory which still stands today. Operating successfully for many years from the Granton base this company made continous wire cloth necessary for the paper making industry

In 1835 William became interested in a paper making business at Kinleith, and he was soon fascinated by the whole paper making process. So much so that he eventually owned several paper making mills throughout the country. However, he still hadn't made the connection between wire and paper.

But soon the connection was made, thanks to a man called John McFarlane. In 1858, an advertisement in the newspapers announced that from now on 'Wm. & Jas. McMurray' would be known as 'Robert McFarlane & Son'. It also stated that the firm made wire cloth, and were 'patentees of the self-acting cylindrical pump washers'. Robert McFarlane was William's bother-in-law, and it was his son John who saw the opportunities that the paper making industry presented. When his father died leaving John in charge, he seized the opportunity.

Soon the Steads Place factory was being fitted out with the latest wire cloth making looms, and the business expanded rapidly. In 1897 John and his second son Arthur approached many wire cloth making companies in Glasgow and Newcastle-upon-Tyne, and suggested that they all get together to form one, large company based in Edinburgh. All the companies agreed, and the United Wire Works

Ltd was formed, with John as the chairman. However, there is little doubt that it was Arthur who masterminded the amalgamation, and drove the firm forward.

In 1925 United Wire moved into the old Madelvic works at Granton. Here the company could expand, manufacturing industrial wire cloth and non-ferrous wire. By 1950 it was using its own furnaces on the site to produce continually cast wire in phosphor bronze and brass.

In 1972 it opened a factory in Livingston, West Lothian for the production of woven synthetics used at the wet end of the paper making process. But the headquarters remained at Granton, and today the company makes wire screens and filters, and is the country's leading manufacturer of woven wire cloth. Its products are used all over the world in such diverse products as high-tech filters in military aircraft, fire screens and even biscuit manufacture. That crisscross pattern seen on many biscuits and papers was probably caused by a conveyor belt made by United Wire.

A B Fleming

In 1852, a man called Andrew Bonar Fleming founded an ink making business in Salamander Street in Leith. At this time, Edinburgh's printing and publishing businesses were flourishing, and Fleming hoped to take advantage of this huge market. He was immediately successful, introducing rosin oil (a by-product of refining turpentine from dead pine wood) into his newspaper and book inks, which made them cheaper but no less effective.

By 1870 it was obvious that the Leith works couldn't cope with the increased demand, so in that year he leased a large area of land from the Duke of Buccleuch at Granton and built a new factory. He also leased Caroline Park, the mansion that stood close to the factory, and based his offices there. By now he was exporting inks all over the world.

They were also manufacturing the raw materials for ink making, and the company's rosin oils, which were refined at Granton from American rosin and marketed as 'Granton Oils', became popular all over the world. Vegetable blacks used to manufacture dense black inks were also made at Granton.

As newspaper and book production grew, so there was a need for even cheaper inks, and AB Fleming looked to the United States for its raw materials. There, ink manufacturers began to use

hydrocarbon oils in place of rosin oil and natural gas black in place of vegetable black. AB Fleming did likewise, and sales of their inks soared yet again. They were manufacturing inks for books, newspapers, fine half tone work, letterpress and lithography, all in a wide range of colours.

The chemical works of AB Fleming & Co which were sited to the west of Caroline Park until the late 1960s

By the end of the nineteenth century the factory and its associated plant occupied more than seven acres. Contemporary photographs, before the gas works were built, show a range of brick buildings enclosed by a high wall, with no less than five tall chimneys rising from them. But such was the competition in the ink industry that between the wars the factory had to be almost rebuilt and equipped with the latest high speed ink mills, giving it the largest capacity for ink manufacture anywhere in the world. However, by 1953 it had to increase its capacity, and again a brand new factory was built. The company had healthy markets in Europe, India, Africa, North America, South America and Australia.

In the early 1960s AB Fleming moved their production to Maybury, and closed down the Granton factory. In February 1963 a fire broke out at Maybury, destroying thousands of gallons of printing ink and damaging expensive machinery. A newspaper report tells of how a store of varnish exploded as firemen approached the building, blowing the roof clean off.

In 1966 AB Fleming moved its offices out of Caroline Park, and in October of that year the Duke of Buccleuch bought it back. Thus the company's long association with Granton came to an end. In about 1972 the whole company was bought over by Croda, an American firm of ink makers, and not long after it shut AB Fleming down completely.

(Above and below) examples of the Caroline range of domestic boilers manufactured at Robert Mushet's Caroline foundry

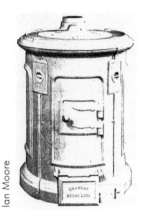

Ian Moore

Caroline Park Foundry

This foundry stood to the north of Granton gas works, next to AB Fleming, and was founded by Robert Mushet, the son of David Mushet, who was born in Dalkeith. He was instrumental in perfecting a method of producing cheap steel called the Bessemer-Mushet process, which involved adding spiegeleisen (molten iron containing magnesium) to the molten metal. He subsequently discovered that by adding a small amount of tungsten he could improve the steel even further. This new metal was called R.M.S., or Robert Mushet's Special Steel, and was the forerunner of today's steels.

However, he never got the recognition he was due for the Bessemer-Mushet Process. Both men initially shared the money they earned from the discovery, but subsequently Bessemer refused to hand over any royalties to Mushet. Mushet took him to court and was awarded £30,000 a year for the rest of his life.

He and his family came to Scotland, setting up a foundry in his father's birthplace of Dalkeith, then another in Leith. His last venture was the Caroline Foundry, which manufactured the 'Caroline' range of domestic cooking and heating equipment. The foundry finally closed down in the 1930s and nothing is left of it.

Ferranti

Ferranti was founded in Oldham in 1896 by Sebastian Zianni de Ferranti, a Liverpudlian. Before that he had been chief electrician to the London Electric Supply Corporation, and was instrumental in setting up the first high voltage power station at Deptford.

By the time he died in Zurich in 1930 he had factories in Lancashire, Canada and the USA manufacturing electric meters, domestic appliances and radio and high voltage electrical equipment. It was the invention of accurate electric meters that made power stations viable, and this was their main product. In the 1930s the company had also been developing instrumentation for aircraft, and in 1942 the company was approached by Sir Stafford Cripps and asked if it would collaborate with government agencies in developing a new aircraft gun sight. Vincent Ferranti agreed, and a new factory was built in Edinburgh, a city which was relatively free from bombing raids.

They chose a green field site at Crewe Toll, and the factory took 18 weeks to build at a cost of £111,000. It was formally opened in

July 1943 with a workforce of 110. By December 1944 this had risen to 950, making it the second largest private employer in Scotland. In 1946 a clock tower was added to the building, and it soon became a well-known Edinburgh landmark. It was demolished in 1999.

After the war, Ferranti flourished. Among its products were the world's first computer-controlled machine tools and the computer-aided drawing machines. In December 1954 a new laboratory complex was opened at Crewe Toll. It was through John (later Sir John) Toothill, the first general manager of Ferranti, and chairman of the Scottish Development Agency, that it was built. One condition placed on it was that the complex had to be used to train electronic engineers for other Scottish companies, and for the next thirty years most electronic companies in Scotland employed staff trained in the laboratories. Some people claim that Scotland's 'Silicon Glen' was founded here.

A Gyro Gun Sight for aircraft made at Ferranti in their new factory at Crewe Toll in 1944

In 1961 new factories were built at Silverknowes and Dalkeith. Vincent (now Sir Vincent) de Ferranti stood down in 1963, and he was succeeded by his son Sebastian. In the same year, the company's football team, Ferranti Thistle, won the East of Scotland Qualifying Cup. It was the first time that a works team had ever won a senior trophy. The team eventually entered the Scottish League as Meadowbank, playing at Meadowbank Stadium, and in the mid 90s moved to Livingston in West Lothian, where it now plays as Livingston FC.

A gun sight under test at Crewe Toll

BAE Systems, Avionics Ltd

The company manufactured many kinds of precision electronic equipment, and was heavily involved in the TSR2 project to build a tactical strike and reconnaissance aircraft for the RAF. Ferranti supplied the radar systems.

In 1968 the company expanded again, this time taking over the old McVitie and Price biscuit factory in Robertson Avenue off Gorgie Road in Edinburgh. It employed over 1,000 people, and brought the total workforce of the company in Scotland to 6,600. This made it the largest private employer of labour in the country.

In 1990, after a merger with, and a fraud by, an American company, Ferranti International went bankrupt. Major parts of the business were sold off to GEC Marconi, and in 1993, exactly fifty years after the company came to Scotland, the 'Ferranti' sign was removed from the Crewe Toll factory and replaced with 'GEC Marconi Avionics'. It is now owned by British Aerospace Europe, which is still on the site.

Tom Ward

The local Bruce Peebles/ Parsons Peebles factory came to a dramatic end in a fire in 1999

Bruce Peebles

Bruce Peebles at one time was one of the main employers in Edinburgh. It has gone through a variety of names in its history, including Parsons Peebles, NEI Peebles, Rolls Royce Peebles Electric and VA Tech Peebles Transformers, the name under which the main business now operates.

It was founded by David Bruce Peebles, who was born in Dundee in 1826. After serving an engineering apprenticeship, he worked in the rail industry in England and France. On his return to Scotland, he designed gas meters for Fullerton & Company in Edinburgh.

In 1866 he set up his own business in Fountainbridge expanded to Bowling Green Street in Leith, where he established the Tay Works. His products included valves, meters and control equipment, and he even experimented with gas engines as a source of generating electricity.

In 1898 the Tay Works were divided into two sections – one for manufacturing gas equipment, and the other for gas engines. The gas engines were so successful that soon they were being installed in generating stations throughout Britain and its colonies, mainly for running tram systems and street lighting.

After Peebles's death in 1899, the company built a new factory in East Pilton, which opened in 1904. It manufactured electrical equipment, while the Leith plant concentrated on gas. The East Pilton factory prospered, and was soon designing and manufacturing motors, generators and high voltage transformer equipment used in the transmission of electricity over long distances.

During World War II it made mobile generators, as well as rocket launchers, submarine engines, searchlights and mortars. One of its main products was hand-held generators for field radios, and over 75,000 were manufactured. The chairman at this time was Sir William Darling, MP for Edinburgh Pentlands, owner of a fashion shop in Princes Street and Lord Provost of the city.

The company prospered after the war, and exported electrical equipment all over the world to be used in power stations. VA Tech, an Austrian company, now owns its transformer department, and Peebles Electric Machines, an Australian company, owns its rotating machinery division. After a disastrous fire at its East Pilton Works in April 1999 the factory was demolished, and the company moved to a new site in Leith, thus cutting its links with Granton.

Other Industries

There were. of course, other industries in Granton. The Granton Ice Company was formed in 1906 to supply ice to the fishing industries of Granton and Newhaven, and in 1921 built a production unit on the Middle Pier of Granton Harbour. It soon expanded and eventually had a large factory on the West Shore Road, close to where Granton Castle once stood. By 1952 it was the most modern factory of its kind in Britain, and could manufacture 100 tons of ice a day whenever necessary.

Within the factory there were rows of moulds, with two dozen to a bank, which were filled with fresh, pure water. Round the moulds water circulated, which had previously been cooled by ammonia expansion. Within 24 hours, this froze the water, giving three and a half tons of ice to a bank.

The company made use of water from the Granton Burn to circulate round the moulds. The water was stored in a pond behind Caroline Park (where the depression in the ground and some of the sluices can still be seen) and piped down to the factory in lead pipes, which still run beneath the modern market garden within Granton Castle's old walled garden.

Another industry was brick making. In July 1933 the Granton Brick Company's new factory was officially opened by Sir Samuel Chapman, the local MP. At that time, its plant could produce 22 bricks a minute, though this eventually rose to 300,000 bricks a week when the plant was in full production.

Malcolm Brechin's was a ship breaker's yard which usually broke up small craft such as fishing vessels. However, one of the biggest jobs it undertook was to break up HMS *Viceroy*, a V&W Class destroyer built during World War I. She spent many years after the War lying on a sandbank, and when the present Duke of Buccleuch served as an ordinary seaman aboard her, one of his duties was to paint her sides. It was then that he discovered that she was held together with nothing more than the paint he was applying. He had to work gingerly, in case he put his foot through the side!

Years later he saw the *Viceroy* being broken up at Brechin's yard, and managed to salvage the brass nameplate from its quarter deck. One of his duties had also been to polish it regularly, and to this day he still owns it.

There were two training units in and around Granton. One was based close to Ferranti's Silverknowes Laboratory (which was actually in Muirhouse), and trained men who worked in the Post Office. The other was set up after World War II on land now occupied by the National Museums of Scotland to train ex-servicemen in building skills. However, both Ferranti and Bruce Peebles has their own apprentice schools and training units as well.

Thomas L Devlin & Sons Ltd was also based in Granton and owned many steam trawlers, as well as a net making factory. And over the years the area has played host to sail makers and riggers, stevedores (such as Young and Leslie, based in the old Customs House on West Harbour Road), ship brokers and shipping agents, shipbuilders such as Hawthorn and Company, small craft builders such as Seaspan and Allen & Co, concrete yacht builders, a roofing material manufacturer (Rubroid, which stood near the ice works in West Shore Road), industrial piping suppliers, coal companies, structural steel companies, fish merchants, a lemonade factory (Trussells, on West Shore Road), timber merchants and sawmill owners, bonded warehouses, tobacco warehouses, blacksmiths and a host of other industries.

Granton Township

The Duke didn't just build a harbour, he built a small township to cater for its needs, and those of its ferry passengers. By the late 1860s it had a population of between 700 and 800, and was centred on what is now Granton Square. But even then there weren't enough workers to cater for all the harbour's needs, and people were commuting from Edinburgh each day.

The Duke instigated an architectural competition to design the township's layout, and a great number of entries were received. The winning design was acknowledged not to be the finest architecturally, but certainly the finest in making use of the available land.

It envisaged stately terraces fronting the sea (no doubt drawing on the terraces of the New Town for inspiration) with a 'fine street running up the centre, and the vista enclosed by a stately church'. A contemporary newspaper account suggests that the Duke was trying to develop, not a working town to serve the harbour, but a resort and watering place. It mentions three classes of houses for three distinct classes of people, 'excellent sea promenades and bathing', a splendid marine view and good rail communications.

Unfortunately, after Granton Square was completed, very little else was built. But the square itself prospered. By 1868 there were wool stores, a building to the west of the pier to accommodate shipping firm offices, the main offices of the harbour company, and a hotel. And just off the square, in West Harbour Road, a customs house (which is still there) was opened in 1862.

The Granton Hotel (built in 1838) was the most important building in the development, and stood to the east of the square, in what later became HMS *Claverhouse*. It was built with ferry passengers in mind, and offered comfortable but not luxurious accommodation. Round the corner, on Lower Granton Road, was the Granton Tavern (known locally as the 'Granton Tap'), which survived as a pub until 1999.

To the east of the hotel were 40 two storey cottages (which are still standing), inhabited by skilled people who worked in the harbour, while the 'labouring classes' were accommodated in temporary structures to the west of the pier.

Ian Moore

The Granton Square Bank Robbery

A branch of the Royal Bank of Scotland had been established in the Square, and was the scene of an infamous armed robbery in 1923. On Friday January 20, at about three in the afternoon, three masked men entered the bank with revolvers and held it up. The staff consisted of a manager, teller and clerk, and one of the robbers threw pepper in their faces while the other two helped themselves to £1779 19s 9d in loose notes and coins.

All three then made their getaway on a motorcycle, with one man at the handlebars and the other two hanging on as best they could. It made its way up Granton Road, turning off into Boswall Road at the top of the hill. The robbery soon became front page news all over the country when the manager, James Dick Main, collapsed and died a few days later of a heart attack. The bank immediately offered a reward of £500 for information leading to the capture of the robbers. However, a Corporation labourer named Kelly, who had been digging a trench in the Square, had noted the motorcycle's

number. He was also sure he could identify one of the men. The motor cycle was found to belong to William Stewart, a Glaswegian. However, he denied being involved in the robbery, and said that he had met with an accident while touring with the motor cycle, and had sold it to a passing lorry driver.

Detective-Lieutenant Sangster of the Edinburgh police sent Kelly to Glasgow, and at an identity parade he was able to identify Stewart as one of the men. A subsequent search of Stewart's house found lots of incriminating evidence, and the motor cycle was recovered from the Clyde, where it had been dumped.

The police eventually made seven arrests, though the charges against three men were dropped. One man stood trial at the High Court in Edinburgh on March 23, and got eight years. On June 12 the others appeared at the High Court in Glasgow. One man was sentenced to fourteen years and two to six months. Most of the money was recovered.

View of Granton from the east breakwater

Sir John Murray

Sir John Murray lived in Challenger Lodge (now part of St Columba's Hospice), which stands in Boswall Place above Lower Granton Road. Strictly speaking, the house (designed by William Henry Playfair in 1825) is in Wardie, but because of his work with the Scottish Marine Station, he is usually associated with Granton.

Sir John was born in Coburg, Canada, of Scottish parents, and returned to Scotland in 1858 when he was 17 years old. The crossing of the Atlantic had a great effect on him, and he arrived in Scotland with a love of the sea. He attended Stirling High School, and then Edinburgh University, though he never graduated. In 1868, with no qualifications, he accepted the post of surgeon aboard the whaler Jan Mayen, which sailed the Arctic. He explored the waters of Spitzbergen (now called Svalbard) and landed on Jan Mayen island, to the north east of Iceland.

But his great chance came when the government decided to equip a vessel that would sail the oceans, conducting oceanographic experiments as it went. Challenger was a corvette of 2306 tons, and was under the direction of Professor (later Sir) Wyville Thomson of Edinburgh University. It first set out in 1872, and aboard was John Murray, taken on as a naturalist at £200 a year. While on board, he soon developed an interest in the 'oozes' and other deposits on the ocean floor.

Over the succeeding years he became an expert on all aspects of the ocean floor, especially coral reefs. With Fred Pullar (son of Laurence Pullar), he even undertook a survey of 562 fresh water lochs in Scotland, though Fred was drowned shortly after the survey got underway.

One of his colleagues was Robert Irvine, and together they embarked on a series of chemical investigations on carbonate of lime secreted by sea organisms, and a series of papers produced by them subsequently appeared in the Proceedings of the Royal Society of Edinburgh. Irvine was also one of the instigators of the Scottish Marine Station.

Sir John Murray was, according to those who knew him, short, broad shouldered, and had piercing blue eyes. He was also domineering, blunt and short tempered, and generally got his own way in everything. Sir Arthur Conan Doyle knew him, and based his character Professor Challenger on him in his book The Lost World. It is said that no one who knew Murray and had read the book failed to see the resemblance between them.

Sir John was killed in a motoring accident in 1914, and now lies buried in Dean Cemetery, Edinburgh.

Scottish Marine Station

At a meeting of the executive committee of the Edinburgh Fisheries Exhibition of 1882, it was resolved that £1600 should be handed over to the Scottish Meteorological Society so that investigations could be carried out on fishing in Scottish waters. Part of the money was to be spent on establishing a marine station somewhere in the country. However, it was discovered that £1600 wasn't enough, and it wasn't until Sir John Murray, a respected oceanographer, offered to equip a such a station on the Firth of Forth that the idea became a reality. An anonymous gentleman, later identified as Lawrence Pullar of the 'Pullars of Perth' family, which owned a chain of dry-cleaning establishments, also pledged £1000, along with various other people and organisations, who contributed in total over £1400. Finally, the Government Grant Committee gave a grant of £520.

A 15 year lease was therefore negotiated with the Duke of Buccleuch for the old Granton Quarry, which had been flooded by the sea in 1855. By 1884 the station (the first of its kind in Britain) was up and running, and consisted of a small floating laboratory aboard the Ark, which was moored in the quarry, a 30 ton steam yacht called Medusa, and a few rowing boats. Some time later laboratories and a small museum were constructed on the shore within a number of 'rough sheds' (some of two storeys) surrounded by brick walls. Also on the shore stood a case for meteorological thermometers and a corrugated iron shed for storing bulky gear.

The Ark was originally a horse barge called Elizabeth which plied the Forth and Clyde Canal. Sir John had the Ark towed from Grangemouth to the shipbuilding yard of Allen & Co in Granton, where a 'house' was built on her to act as a workroom and laboratory.

In the Firth of Forth twelve stations were laid down on the charts between Alloa and the Isle of May where temperatures were taken on the surface of the water, at intermediate depths and on the bottom. Water samples were also taken for analysis throughout the year. The deepest water in the Firth of Forth (40 fathoms) is found just above the Forth Bridge, and there temperatures were taken at 5 fathom depths.

The Medusa, however, didn't just sail the on the Firth of Forth. She also ventured out into the North Sea, with Sir John Murray, as well as JT Cunningham, superintendent of the marine station, carrying out various experiments. But she was found to be unsuitable for open waters, and in 1884 was towed through the Forth and Clyde Canal to the Firth of Clyde, which was more sheltered. The following year she formed the basis of another marine station inspired by Sir John at Port Loy, Millport, on the Isle of Cumbrae.

A contemporary description of the laboratory on the Ark states that the after-room could accommodate four people, and was fitted out for microscope work. The outer room, which was 20 feet long, had a table running the full length of its south side where aquaria were positioned. One third of the table was fitted with a marble slab, one third was plate glass, and the other third had tiles of various tints so that experiments on the effect of colour on marine animals and plants could be conducted. A number of taps along the table's length supplied sea water for the scientists, fed from a tank on the roof of the lighter, into which sea water was pumped. Sir John, at his own expense, also rented Inchcolm, the island in the Firth of Forth, where there was a house where various other experiments could be conducted.

The object of the station was to examine the Firth of Forth and the neighbouring seas 'from a biological, physical and chemical point of view'. It also proposed to investigate the life-history of marine forms, and their relation to their surrounding conditions. However, there were no arrangements for keeping marine animals of any size on the station for any length of time.

One of the main problems to be investigated by the station was the disappearance of the once productive oyster beds in the Firth of Forth. It was by no means certain that they had disappeared through over-fishing, and one theory was that 'spat' (the spawn of the oyster) was being destroyed by unfavourable weather conditions. However, there was no hatchery for oysters at the station, so investigating the oyster population proved impossible.

The marine station didn't survive for long. There was always a shortage of money, and staff left for more lucrative posts with alarming regularity. It was also found that the waters of the west coast were richer in marine life, so work tended to be concentrated there. In 1903, less than twenty years after it was founded, the station closed down.

Life in Granton

Pilton Housing Schemes

Before the building of the housing schemes at East and West Pilton, the area between the railway line north of Ferry Road and West Granton Road was largely farmland. A map dated 1930 shows that only the area south of Wardie Crescent and east of Boswall Terrace was being developed, with the main thoroughfare being Boswall Drive.

The map also shows four farms – Granton Mains (on West Granton Road, opposite the gas works); Royston Mains (which was the home farm for Caroline Park at one time) on West Granton Road, close to the junction with present-day Royston Mains Road; East Pilton Farm, near where Pilton Place now meets Pilton Avenue; and West Pilton, close to the corner of West Pilton Avenue and Pennywell

Ian Moore

West Pilton Farm around 1912
The farmer or his grieve, presumably the man with the Homburg, is overseeing the wailing of the season's potato crop. All the women workers are wearing 'uglies' (removable sunshades) and 'brots' (aprons made from discarded sacks). It appears that this photograph was taken where West Pilton Bank and View now are

Road. A fifth farm, called Windlestrawlee, stands south of Boswall Avenue, on the Ferry Road side of the railway line. It played no part in the development of the schemes, and was still there in 1938. It stood on the site now occupied by Ferryfield.

A drawing in *Old and New Edinburgh Volume 3*, published in the nineteenth century, shows East Pilton Farm to have been a prosperous looking place, with a solid, whitewashed, two-storey cottage along with byres and outbuildings, and at least one small farm labourer's cottage, all surrounded by walls and fencing.

In the early 1930s the rest of East Pilton was built, and in 1936-37 work started on West Pilton (divided from East Pilton by the former railway line). By 1938 most of the area was developed as housing, though a map of that year shows that most parts of West Pilton were still to be built, and indeed work was not completed on them until after World War II. West Pilton Farm was still standing, and three reservoirs are clearly marked, in that area enclosed by present-day West Pilton Green, West Pilton Lea and West Pilton Drive. Indeed, West Pilton Loan goes right through where they were located.

The majority of the housing was council housing, built by the old Edinburgh Corporation, and the majority of its tenants came from Leith, with a small percentage coming from the slums of the Old Town. East Pilton had a good mix of houses and flats, and considered itself superior to West Pilton, which was mainly flats and maisonettes. East Pilton was also perceived as having the best facilities as far as shops, churches and other amenities were concerned.

But East Pilton itself had two areas that were perceived to be 'inferior' and 'superior' by those living there, and the dividing line was Boswall Parkway, which at one time was known as 'Snob Alley'. The area to the north was almost wholly council housing, while the area to the south – the so-called 'superior' area – was private rented housing built by McTaggart and Mickel. They became known as the 'Gumley' houses, named after their factor, and consisted mainly of four flats in a block, with bay windows and shingles between the upstairs and downstairs windows.

However, all of East and West Pilton was perceived as a desirable place to live when it was first built, as the housing was infinitely better than the slums from which many of the tenants came. The inhabitants saw themselves as what used to be called the 'aspiring working class' – having a good trade, engineering skills, or a job in a shop of office. It has been claimed that East Pilton is the best designed of all the Edinburgh council schemes. It was planned as a 'garden suburb', with gardens surrounding every house or tenement, and all the facilities needed by an area close to hand.

In 1954 East Pilton was chosen as the first area in Scotland to have a mass X-ray trial scheme. Many TB patients were identified through this, and the women of the area started a support group for the families. This led to a campaign for a community centre in Royston/Wardieburn, and this in turn led to the community action groups in the Granton and Greater Pilton area.

But things started to go wrong in the area in the 1970s, when unemployment began to rise. Local industry went into decline, and job opportunities became fewer. This accelerated in the 1980s, when money to refurbish council housing dried to a trickle. Coupled to this was the 'right to buy' legislation, which, while no bad thing in itself, meant that good quality stock was sold off, leaving housing that needed money spent on it.

Then the drug culture arrived. Rightly or wrongly, Pilton and its neighbour Muirhouse were perceived as having an insurmountable drug problem. The truth is that not all of the area was involved, though there were enough drugs around to cause a serious problem.

Once a place is down, it has a tremendous struggle to raise itself once more. Since the early 1990s however, West and East Pilton have risen to the challenge, undergoing a significant regeneration. Some of the older buildings have been pulled down, and the council has gradually been refurbishing those that are left. New projects are underway to create a feeling of community and belonging, and the Granton Housing Association has been promoting and building new houses for sale and rent.

At last people are beginning to perceive the whole Granton area as a desirable place in which to live once more, and this will be accelerated with the creation of Waterfront Edinburgh, a development and marketing agency charged with regenerating the area.

Ian Moore

The Embassy Cinema, fondly remembered by many Granton people, stood in Boswall Parkway, and was opened in 1937. Its final films when it closed in 1964 were The Day of the Triffids and The Legion's Last Patrol

Literary and Artistic Associations

The novelist and short story writer Fred Urquhart lived for some time at 37 West Cottages, Granton, and he used the location in his novel *Time Will Knit*, published in 1938. West Cottages stood between the Middle and West Piers, and were pulled down before World War II. For some time he also lived in Fraser Grove in East Pilton, at two different addresses.

He was born in Eglinton Crescent near St Mary's Cathedral in 1912, and moved to Granton when he was seven years old. After leaving school at fifteen, he worked in a bookshop in Teviot Place, and then for a firm of tailors. In his long literary career, he was a literary agent in London, a scout for Walt Disney and a reader for MGM film studio. In 1989 he returned to Edinburgh, and died in 1995.

And though Boswall Road is, strictly speaking, not in Granton, the well known poet and essayist Alexander Smith lived in a house there for several years, dying in 1867 when only 37 years old. He was born in Kilmarnock, and perhaps his most famous poem was *Life Drama*.

West Pilton and Muirhouse housing schemes were the setting for Irvine Welsh's stark novel of Edinburgh life, *Trainspotting* (1993). He was born in Leith in 1958, and knew the city's housing schemes well, as up until the success of *Trainspotting*, he worked as a training officer for the then Edinburgh District Council's housing department.

There was never a thriving artistic community in Granton. However, since the late 1970s north Edinburgh has played a significant part in the community arts movement in the city as a whole. A number of organisations have existed during that time, including the Pilton Central Association in the 1980s, the Triangle Arts Centre, Muirhouse Festival Association, and the Greater Pilton Design Resource. Currently, the major promoter of the arts in the area is North Edinburgh Arts, which opened a multi media arts centre in 2002. In this context, 'arts' means everything to do with artistic endeavour. The remit of North Edinburgh Arts is to offer social, recreational and educational opportunities to the whole community.

Between 1937 and 1964, Granton had a building where a very popular art form took place. The Embassy Cinema, fondly remembered by many Granton people, stood in Boswall Parkway, and perhaps its finest hour was when Yehudi Menuhin the violinist played there in 1959 during the Edinburgh International Festival.

The cinema was owned by the Miller-McLoughlan group, and opened on August 2 1937. Its first film was *Libelled Lady* starring Spencer Tracy, Myrna Loy, William Powell and Jean Harlow. There was a twice weekly change of programme (on Mondays and Thursdays), and a popular Saturday morning matinee for children. It closed on March 6 1964, soon after a seat fire, with the final films being *The Day of the Triffids* and *The Legion's Last Patrol*.

After closure there were plans to turn it into a dance or a bingo hall, but these came to nothing. Eventually it was demolished in 1975.

National Museums of Scotland planned new public access building

The National Museums of Scotland

The National Museums of Scotland are located at six centres throughout the country. The Museum of Scotland and the Royal Museum are at Chambers Street in Edinburgh, the Museum of Flight is at East Fortune in East Lothian, the Museum of Scottish Country Life is at East Kilbride, the Museum of Costume is at New Abbey in Kirkcudbrightshire, the National War Museum is at Edinburgh Castle, and the museums' store, called the Granton Centre, is at Granton.

It is the main storage centre for those items in the museums' collections that are not on display at any of the other centres. It stands on a twelve acre site which originally formed part of the

© Ken Barry Photography

An aerial view of Edinburgh Waterfront
site looking west to east, showing
Muirhouse, in the foreground, West and
East Piltton

Caroline Park policies, owned by the Duke of Buccleuch. In 1907 he passed it to his son, the Earl of Dalkeith, and it was later sold to Sir James Miller for housing. In 1942 however, most of the site was requisitioned by the government, and in 1946 it became a building trades training centre for ex-servicemen. During the 1950s some of the buildings were also used by local companies, such as Ferranti.

The National Museums moved onto the site in 1975, with one of the buildings being used as a centre for conservation and analytical research. Gradually, over the years, the National Museums took over more of the buildings, and by 1990 occupied the site completely.

Though many of the Granton buildings still date from the time it was a training centre, a new building costing over £6m was opened in 1996, providing 8000 square metres of storage space and the largest conservation laboratories and workshops in Scotland. With the advent of Waterfront Edinburgh, some of the twelve acres, which was surplus to requirements, was released for redevelopment.

But though it is a storage centre, people will have access to the main building, either through open days or by appointment. There will also be displays highlighting the conservation techniques used on the objects in the collection.

National Galleries of Scotland

The National Galleries of Scotland are all situated in and around Edinburgh. There are four main ones – the National Portrait Gallery, the Gallery of Modern Art at Belford Road, the Dean Gallery, and the National Gallery of Scotland on the Mound. There are also two 'partnership' galleries outwith Edinburgh, one at Duff House in Banffshire, and one in Paxton House in Berwickshire.

Although the National Museums of Scotland have had a presence at Granton since 1975, the National Galleries of Scotland will be a new addition to the area, and will have a secure store for paintings and sculpture not shown in any of their other galleries. It is located within the National Museums site, with the National Galleries having taken out a 25 year lease on it. The building housing the collection will cost £2.1m, and like the National Museums building, it will be open to the public on one day each week, and at other times by appointment.

The paintings will not be hung on walls, but in specially constructed racks, and there will be an exhibition area also, where exhibitions of sculpture and photography, and even frame making, will be held from time to time. The collection, it is envisaged, will be an eclectic mix of portraiture, still life, modernist, landscape, sculpture and so on, and a visit will almost be like 'going behind the scenes'.

The Churches

Granton, up until the late 1880s, had been part of the parish of Cramond, and it was to services in that village's church that people went every Sunday. But as the population grew, it was soon realised that it needed a church of its own. So the Rev James Robertson of the Church of Scotland began holding services in an upper room of Granton school until a new church had been built by the Duke of Buccleuch.

Granton Congregational Church, Boswall Parkway

This new church opened in 1877, and still stands at the foot of Granton Road, just off Granton Square, though it is no longer used as a place of worship. The Duke donated it to the Church of Scotland, along with an endowment of £50 a year. In 1889 Granton was detached from Cramond, and became a *'quoad sacra'* (or ecclesiastical) parish in its own right. This new parish also took in parts of the parishes of Dean and St Bernard's.

But this wasn't the first church in the area. In September 1874, a group of men had met at the home of Mr Angus Kennedy in Wardie Crescent to discuss the building of a Free Church to serve the communities in Wardie and Granton. Prior to this, the Rev William Fraser of Free St Bernard's had been conducting open air services in Granton Square every Sunday evening.

The outcome of the meeting was a decision to lease a plot of land at the south-western corner of Granton Road and Wardie Crescent from the Lawson Nursery Company. The nursery agreed, and a kit-form corrugated iron church seating 400 was erected on the site within six weeks. It cost £625, and was put up by Crosson & Company of London.

However, the Free Church looked upon it as a 'preaching station' rather than a fully fledged church, even though a minister, the Rev AS Paterson, had been appointed to conduct services at a stipend of £100 a year. In 1875 it was decided to extend the 'mission' aspect of the church by conducting services in a room in Caroline Park, at that time leased by ink manufacturers AB Fleming. This was for those families living in the Quarriers' Cottages on what is now West Shore Road.

St Paul's RC Church, Muirhouse Avenue

Eventually, in 1876, the church became a full congregation of the Free Church. But it was still housed in a corrugated iron building, and members of the congregation were pressing for something more church-like and permanent. Consequently, in 1878 it was decided to buy a plot of land on Ferry Road, at the top of Granton Road, from the Fettes Trust.

In 1880 work began on the new building, and it was formally opened on June 3 1881. It cost £5,000, with £325 of this coming from the sale of the corrugated iron church to a Congregational church in Berwick-upon-Tweed. So the Granton and Wardie Free Church moved out of the area, and was renamed St James Free Church. However, the area it served still included Granton, as well as Ferry Road as far as Goldenacre, Trinity and Wardie.

Granton Parish Church, Boswall Parkway

In 1900 the Free Church of Scotland came together with the United Presbyterian church to form the United Free Church, Then, in October 1929, the United Free Church amalgamated with the Church of Scotland, and St James became simply 'Inverleith Parish Church'.

Meanwhile, new housing was being built on the farmlands of East and West Pilton, and while Inverleith Church could cope with the increased population, the small Church of Scotland building at Granton Square could not. It was also in the wrong position to serve this new community. So, in the early 1930s the Home Mission of the Church of Scotland acquired land on Boswall Parkway, and work began on a new church, the architect being John F Matthew.

The foundation stone was laid on October 22 1934 by the Duke of York (later George VI). A casket was laid beneath the stone in which was placed a *Scotsman* newspaper, a copy of *Life and Work*, extension scheme documents, the architect's description of the church, the names of those involved in its building, a note of its overall cost and a copy of the programme for the stone-laying ceremony. The whole church was completed by 1936, and on February 26 of that year it was dedicated by the Moderator of the General Assembly, the Rt Rev Marshall Lang.

The church was the fifth to be built in Edinburgh under the Church of Scotland National Extension Scheme, and is said to be the most beautiful. The hewn stone is from Doddington Quarry in Northumberland, while the rubble facework is from Edinburgh's own Craigmillar Quarry. The ceiling is of ash and cedar, the aisle and chancel floors of polished birch, and the eastern wall is panelled in oak. The apse seating, pulpit, choir stalls, lectern and font are also in oak.

Other denominations were considering churches as well. The Salvation Army opened a hall in 1935 in Wardieburn Drive, and it was rebuilt in 1995. It consists of a main church hall, which can hold 80, a community hall, where 40 people can sit for a meal, and a vestibule. The Salvation Army has taken part in many Granton initiatives over the years, and at present is involved in a kids' community programme. Every year the children visit local old folks' homes and hold carol services with tambourines, which is very popular.

The Congregational Church was opened in 1936. At an assembly in Dundee in 1935, it had decided to embark on a church extension scheme to cater for the new housing that was being built in Scotland at the time, and the first one built was in Granton. A site on Boswall Parkway was bought, and the finished church was opened and dedicated on September 9 1936. The architect was FW MacDonald of Clydebank, and the building material was a synthetic stone called 'Coltmuir'. It could seat 458 people, with the hall seating 244, and cost £3000.

St Margaret Mary's RC Church

The foundation stone of the Methodist Church in Boswall Parkway was laid on September 25 1937. However, to find the church's origins we must go back to a mission called Wesley Hall set up in Stockbridge many years before. Its earliest records date from 1876.

It was an active mission, and by the beginning of the twentieth century was holding, in addition to church services, open air prayer meetings in Inverleith Park every Saturday evening. But over the years money was a problem, and when it was discovered in 1936 that the mission would need a new roof within the next five years, it was decided to abandon it. By this time a committee of the Methodist Church had decided that churches should be built in the new housing schemes that were springing up. It seemed logical, therefore, for the Stockbridge mission to move to East Pilton, where there was already a Methodist Boys' Club. At least two Granton men – Daniel Paterson and David Archer – went on to become Methodist ministers.

The Roman Catholic Church opened in 1939 on Boswall Parkway to serve a rapidly expanding Catholic population in Granton. It was dedicated to St Margaret Mary, a French nun of the Visitation convent at Paray-le-Monial, who lived between 1647 and 1690, and who had revelations and visions of Christ. She was canonised by Pope Benedict XV in 1920.

Seen from the outside, the church looks small and plain, but this is deceiving. The inside is light and spacious, and almost as wide as it is long. Above the main windows on each side are small stained glass windows dedicated to various saints, from St Andrew and St Ninian to St Kentigern and St George. These were donated by various families in Granton who had helped found the church.

While St David's Roman Catholic School was being built in the late 1930s, temporary classes were held in the church, the two side areas being curtained off to give a number of classrooms. The fourteen Stations of the Cross within the church are by Felix McCulloch, a local artist, and the painting of Christ at the back of the church was by an art master at Fettes College.

In 1999 a small convent dedicated to St Margaret of Scotland was established next to St Margaret Mary's presbytery for two or three nuns of the Franciscan Sisters of the Immaculate Conception.

The Old Kirk, Church of Scotland, Pennywell Road

The Edinburgh Baptist Association initiated pioneering work in the north of Edinburgh just before World War II. Within eighteen months of its first service being held in a local scout hut, Granton Baptist Church, known affectionately as 'The Hut', was opened on July 9 1940. In December 1952 a more permanent church was opened, with some of the money coming from the sale of the Marshall Street Church in the city centre. The minister of that church was the Rev Francis Johnstone, and he is remembered in the official name of Granton Baptist Church – the 'Francis Johnstone Memorial'. A new hall was added in 1972, and a new sanctuary costing £350,000 twenty years later.

The Scottish Episcopalian Church established a place of worship in Royston Mains Place in 1941 as a mission church, and dedicated to St David of Scotland. It was formally opened and dedicated on June 18 by Bishop Logie Danson of Edinburgh. There had been Episcopalian services held in Granton before this. The first recorded service was in the house occupied temporarily by the Rev GCC Wilson the priest-in-charge at 30 Boswall Green, on February 23 1941.

Later, the church became a lively centre for worship and social events. Many concerts and dances were held, and as there was no hall at that time, the dance band set up in the sanctuary and the church seating was moved back against the walls.

But there was still no priest's house, and one of the sights of Granton was to see the priest and his curate motorcycling from Boswall Green to Royston Mains Place, their cassocks flapping in the wind. So, in 1950, a church house was built (later called 'St David's House', or 'The Friary'), as was a hall.

In the 1960s the church became famous for its Christmas pantomimes, written by the then priest, Rev Chris Porteus. They were performed at Ainslie Park School, and attracted hundreds of people.

In the 1970s, under the Rev Bob Sinclair, the 'men in brown' arrived in Granton. These were monks from the Anglican Society of St Francis, and they are still fondly remembered to this day. They first lived in two flats in Royston Mains Place before moving into The Friary. However, in 1985 they decided they could best carry out their work in Edinburgh from a central location, and they moved out of Granton. The Friary was demolished and replaced by the Crewe Toll Medical Centre, and in 2000 the hall was also demolished and the Centre extended. By the year 2000 the church had no regular priest-in-charge, and the services were congregation-led. The present priest-in-charge (appointed in May 2002) is the Rev David Durie, a Granton man who returned to the area after nineteen years away.

Granton Methodist Church, Boswall Parkway

The Church of Scotland 'Old Kirk' (known locally as the 'White Kirk') in Pennywell Road has its origins in the Reformation. John Knox had become minister of St Giles, and in 1598 the city was divided into four districts. The church was adapted to provide four areas where each district could worship separately. The people from the south east of the city worshipped in what was called the 'Old Kirk', located in the central part of St Giles.

In 1869 St Giles became one church again, and three congregations moved out. The Old Kirk occupied a number of buildings before a new church was built for it at the corner of St John's Street and Holyrood Road. On January 3 1941 it moved to Crewe Toll (where the Shell garage now stands), and in 1950 the foundation stone was laid for the present Old Kirk. It opened for worship on November 25 1951. A wooden hall was built in 1960, but this burnt down ten years later. The new halls were built in 1972.

Most of the Granton churches got together in the 1970s to form Granton Churches Together, a local group of Action of Churches Together in Scotland, or ACTS. In this way the many churches in the area (and Granton is unusual in having so many active churches in such a small area) can serve the parish together rather than in competition. Each year they hold a Good Friday walk, starting off at Granton Baptist Church and ending up at the Salvation Army Goodwill Centre, which the organisers claim has the 'best kitchen for hot soup'.

In the year 2000 the Congregational Church became a congregation within the Northern Synod of the United Reformed Church. Then, in June 2002, both it and the Methodist Church came together to form the Granton United Church. The congregations worship together in the same building under a shared minister and elders' council.

Education

Before the arrival of Granton Harbour and its associated developments, the children of the area – mostly the sons and daughters of farmers and farm labourers – had to walk to the parish school in Cramond to receive an education. In 1885 the Duke of Buccleuch had a school built just off Granton Square (the architect being Robert Wilson), and paid £150 a year for its upkeep. Formerly known as the 'board school', it still stands on the south side of West Granton Road, and is now used as a youth centre.

The original Granton School at Granton Square

When East and West Pilton were being developed, it was realised that the school was in the wrong place to cater for the influx of children. Consequently, in 1933, a new school was built in Boswall Parkway to replace it. This became Granton Primary School, which is still in existence today.

Its design is similar to four other schools built in Edinburgh at the time. But when built it was unique in one respect – it had the biggest playground of any school in the city, even though a branch library took up some of the area. In fact, the playground was so big that in the year 2000 about a quarter to a third was turned into an 'urban forest' in conjunction with the Forestry Commission. Over 1000 trees were planted.

As the population expanded, so other primary schools opened – Royston and St David's in 1937, Craigmuir in 1951 Pirniehall in 1967 and Inchview in 1974. St David's classes were first held in St Margaret Mary's Church and the old 'board school' at Granton Square before moving to its present building in 1951-52. Inchview was built on the playground of the old Pennywell School.

Pennywell School had what was probably the most unusual history of any school in the area. It was founded just before World War II to serve West Pilton, and started off life in blocks of council flats at 676, 678, 680 and 682 Ferry Road and 696, 698, 700 and 702 Ferry Road. For a while 702 even housed the school dentist. Also part of the school were the flats at 3, 5, 7 and 9 Ferry Road Avenue. The headmaster, Mr Davie, used number 3 as his office, and the janitoress, Mrs Morgan, lived upstairs in number 5. The school library was in the front room of what is now 676 Ferry Road. In 1948 the school relocated to West Pilton Avenue.

Over the years the population of Granton has been dropping, and this has meant a drop in pupil numbers. In 2002 St David's relocated to a new campus at Pirniehall School at West Pilton Crescent. Both schools remained autonomous, though they shared many of the facilities. In 2003 Inchview and Craigmuir will move, and share a new campus in the old St David's site.

Up until 1991 Granton had its own comprehensive school – Ainslie Park (formerly West Pilton Junior Secondary School). It opened in 1949, with its first head teacher being Dr Norman Murchison, a descendant of the Scotsman who had given his name to the Murchison Falls on the Nile in Uganda. The school building had actually been started in the late 1930s, but was abandoned because of the war.

Due to falling pupil numbers, it amalgamated with Broughton High School, and Telford College took over the buildings as its northern campus. Nowadays secondary education is provided by Broughton High School on East Fettes Avenue, south of Ferry Road, and Craigroyston Community High School.

Telford College, previously Ainslie Park High School

Craigroyston opened in 1963, and though it sits in Muirhouse, it still has a large influence on the Granton area. It was one of the first schools in Edinburgh to be given 'community' status, which means that it is looked upon as a community asset as well as a school, playing host to lots of clubs, sporting activities and evening classes.

In December 1919 the site that the school now occupies hosted an unusual event – a flying circus. Cobham's Air Carnival took people on joy trips over the city, and an account in the *Edinburgh Evening News* of December 29 states that 'Cobham's Air Carnival was greeted most enthusiastically by a large and appreciative audience'.

It wasn't until 1968 that further education came to the Granton area, with the opening of Telford College, named after Thomas Telford, one of Scotland's most famous civil engineers. But to find its true origins we must go back to 1874, when the Abbeyhill Heriot School was opened at the junction of Easter Road, Montrose Terrace and West Norton Place at Calton. In 1886 it was taken over by the Edinburgh School Board as a mixed school, and renamed the Regent Road Public School.

In 1894 it began offering evening classes, the first tentative step towards further education in the city. Within a month 100 pupils had enrolled, studying such subjects as arithmetic, English, book-keeping and dressmaking. Soon French, singing, needlework and more vocational subjects such as shorthand were being added to the curriculum.

Granton School, Boswall Parkway

So successful was it that by 1903 over 28 Edinburgh schools were offering similar night classes, along with established colleges such as Heriot Watt, Edinburgh College of Art, Edinburgh and East of Scotland

College of Agriculture and the Edinburgh School of Cookery and Domestic Economy. The Tynecastle Supplementary School and Workshops were subsequently opened in 1914 at Gorgie, and here, for the first time, vocational classes could be offered in such skills as metalworking, building, plasterwork and tailoring.

Meanwhile, the Regent Road School continued to offer evening classes, though in 1955 it was taken over by the Regent Road Day Institute. By the late 1940s, however, it had become apparent that further education in Edinburgh – and throughout Scotland – was in need of overhaul. A suggestion was made that two 'advanced-level' colleges and four 'craft-level' colleges should be built. The two advanced-level colleges were to be Napier (later to become Napier University), and the College of Commerce. However, only three craft-level colleges were built – Telford, Stevenson and Esk Valley.

A principal for Telford was appointed in 1966, before the college was built, and it operated out of various buildings dotted round the city, including the Regent Road Day Institute. However, on August 26 1968 – a year later than planned – the Crewe Toll campus opened for business. The final cost was over £1.5m, with Edinburgh Corporation putting in £273,000 of this.

Over the years, the college has expanded. In 1991 it took over the old Ainslie Park Secondary School as a northern campus. In 1993 the college was taken out of education authority control and became an incorporated body, and it remains so today. In 2005 it will move to SecondSite's former gasworks land within the Granton redevelopment area, drawing all the departments together in one dedicated campus offering a superb environment for study and learning.

Northern General Hospital

Northern General Hospital, now demolished

This stood at the corner of Ferry Road and Pilton Drive. Its origins go back to the time when Leith traded with ports all over Europe, especially those on the Baltic coast. This brought prosperity to Leith, but it also brought diseases like cholera and typhus, carried by the ships' crews.

The town did have some contingencies for this kind of thing, though they were very basic. Houses at Coalhill, Water Street and Broad Wynd were used as temporary hospitals, and there was even a wooden hospital built on Leith Links, which was run as a charity.

None of these were satisfactory, and the citizens of the town were unhappy that some of the beds were being taken up by foreigners. Another concern was that patients with injuries or minor illnesses were often put in beds beside patients with infectious diseases. Many people died after cross infection, and the wooden hospital soon gained the nickname of the 'Killing Hoose'. Patients much preferred to be taken to the Royal Infirmary in Edinburgh, even though the trip there took place in an uncomfortable wooden cart.

Emigration to America was in full swing in the nineteenth century. Some emigrants from the Baltic countries would first sail to Leith, then travel overland to the Clyde ports, where they finally embarked for the New World. Those who had taken ill on board the ships sailing to Leith inevitably found themselves in the Leith hospital, adding to the strain on its resources.

Leith Town Council therefore decided to build a new fever hospital away from the densely populated areas of the town. In 1894 it purchased a site at East Pilton, and the town architect, James Simpson, was instructed to design the building. But there was apprehension about the scheme. The trustees of Fettes College, well to the south, opposed the hospital, and only relented when the Council agreed to build an avenue of trees south of Ferry Road to act as a barrier. That 'barrier' is still there, testimony to the ignorance of some late Victorians about infectious diseases.

The hospital was opened on September 11 1896 by John Bennet, the Provost of Leith, and called the 'Leith Public Health Hospital'. It had four single isolation wards with square corner pavilions for ward offices, an administration block, and a gate house, all of red brick. The administration block was an impressive building, with two ornate coat-of-arms carved on stones on either side of the main entrance. One showed the Lion Rampant, and one showed Leith's coat-of-arms and motto. Above the door was a further carved stone commemorating the official opening. It read:

Leith Public Health Hospital

Erected 1894 - 1896

Opened 11th Sept. 1896. John Bennet, Provost

In 1929 the hospital came under the control of Edinburgh Corporation, along with St Cuthbert's and the former Leith Poor House. In 1932 they became the Northern, Western and Eastern General Hospitals. At the beginning of World War II the Northern became the Edinburgh Poorhouse for two years, and afterwards the facilities built for them (to the west of the hospital) were used to house and treat wounded servicemen. These servicemen had a uniform of royal blue blazer, grey flannels, white shirt and red tie. The facilities were eventually closed down, and the wards became file stores.

In 1995 the hospital closed down, and eventually demolished. A supermarket now occupies the site.

Edinburgh City FC

Edinburgh City
pictured in 1930.
The club folded in the early
1950s

Over the years, Edinburgh has had many football teams in the Scottish League. Apart from the present-day Heart of Midlothian and Hibernian, there were four others – St Bernards (which played in Broughton), Leith Athletic, Meadowbank Thistle (now relocated to Livingston) and Edinburgh City. Of these, perhaps Edinburgh City has the most interesting story, and not just because its ground was close to Granton.

It was the smallest of the Edinburgh clubs, and was founded in 1928 with the best of intentions. It was to be an amateur team, the same as Queen's Park in Glasgow, and would give an outlet for those young men in Edinburgh who wanted to play at the highest level but were not interested in earning money through it. In honour of Queen's Park, its colours were black and white.

The founding fathers were Councillor JR Coltart, Bailie W McLaren and Mr GH Mitchell. To begin with it played in the East of Scotland League, sharing with Leith Athletic a ground at Marine Gardens for its home games. Without a track record of success, in May 1931 it applied for membership of the old Second Division of the Scottish League, but was turned down. Teams from Bo'ness and Clydebank were admitted instead. Clydebank eventually resigned after only a few months, and Edinburgh City replaced it.

It was a peculiar decision on behalf of the League, as Edinburgh City had only been in existence for three years. Not only that, this gave Edinburgh five senior teams at a time when some of the others were struggling to attract acceptable crowds. No doubt the League was swayed by the romantic notion of a team which put sportsmanship above money.

The directors enthusiastically set about making plans for the future, and the first thing they did was move the club from Marine Gardens to the new Powderhall Stadium. However, this first season in the Scottish league was not a success. Out of 38 games played, it managed to win only five and draw seven. Defeats of 6-0 were not unknown.

However, it was reselected into the League the following season. By 1933 a pattern had been established – Edinburgh City would end the season at the bottom of the League while still managing to gain admittance to the League for a further year. During the 1934-35 season it moved back to Marine Gardens, and from there to City Park, later renamed East Pilton Park (which bore no relation to the present day East Pilton Park).

It stood (and indeed parts of it still stand) in Pilton Drive, close to its junction with Ferry Road, and opposite the present-day Safeway supermarket. This was its first true home, and the first match to take place there was on August 12 1935. Not unnaturally, it was a defeat at the hands of newly relegated Falkirk before a crowd of 1000 hardy souls. By the sixth match of the season, Edinburgh City had climbed up to sixth bottom, the highest place it would ever achieve in the League.

City Park,
later named East Pilton Park

Perhaps their finest hour was a cup match played during the 1938-39 season, when, before a crowd of nearly 9000 supporters, it defeated Hibs 3-2 at Easter Road. However, the following cup match saw a return to form when City were beaten 9-2 by Raith Rovers at Starks Park.

After World War II the Scottish League was reformed, though Edinburgh City played no part in it. Instead, it played in the Eastern League (which lasted only one season). Even here it was not particularly successful, with the gate receipts for one game against East Stirling amounting to only £1.50.

When it was announced that the Scottish League would consist of three divisions during the 1946-47 season, it applied to join Division 'C', where some of the top teams' reserve sides played, and was successful. But again it ended up at the foot of the table. However, it reapplied for the 1947-48 season, and got back in. They finished second bottom.

The 1948-49 season was to be their last in senior football. In a desperate attempt to bring some experience to the side, they turned professional, but it did no good. The following season saw them in the Edinburgh and District Junior League, and even here their performance was poor. The team finally folded in 1955, though in 1986 the name was revived when a Post Office team called itself Edinburgh City.

In truth, the club was not so much a Granton team as an Edinburgh team which happened to have its ground close to Granton. But it must have drawn some of its support (such as it was) from the newly built Pilton housing schemes, and it did discover one of Scotland's most famous players – Willie Bauld, who later went on to play for Hearts and Scotland.

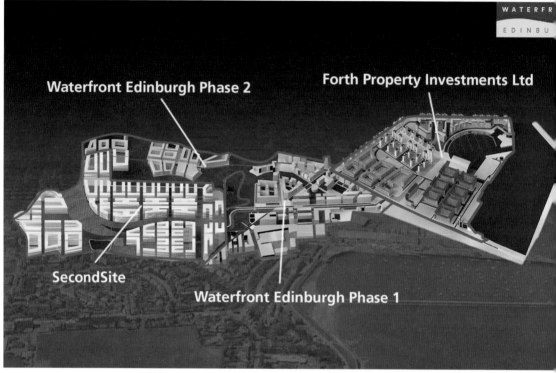

A still from a Virtual Reality Model of the project showing major land ownership

Waterfront Edinburgh

Throughout the 70s, 80s and 90s Granton was in decline. Its traditional industries either closed down or moved away, the harbour saw little commercial activity, and the rail links to the centre of the city had closed down long ago. The area was scarred and derelict, and seemed to have no role to play in the future of Edinburgh.

But there was no denying its superb location. It lay along the shores of the Firth of Forth, with wonderful views across to Fife and upriver to the two Forth Bridges, and it was no more than two miles from the city centre. This made it one of the prime redevelopment sites in Europe, and it wasn't long before people saw its vast potential. In March 2000 a new publicly funded body called Waterfront Edinburgh Ltd was established to develop and market an area extending to over 140 hectares (346 acres).

This joint venture company was set up by the City of Edinburgh Council and Scottish Enterprise Edinburgh & Lothian with the aim of creating a second 'New Town' which would be a mix of business, leisure and tourism facilities, commerce and residential communities.

Waterfront Edinburgh Ltd is one of three major landowners, each of which owns or controls just over 40 hectares (about 100 acres), with the balance in smaller parcels. Moving from east to west, Granton Harbour is owned by Forth Property Investments Ltd; Waterfront Edinburgh is the principal landowner in the central part; and SecondSite Holdings Ltd owns the former gasworks to the west of the site.

The life of the project is reckoned to be between twelve and fifteen years. During that time some 6,500 homes will be built, and between 14,000 and 17,000 jobs (of which 9,000 will be new) created. It will be a living, rather than a dormitory, community, with shops, restaurants, pubs and bars, industries, leisure facilities and tourist attractions.

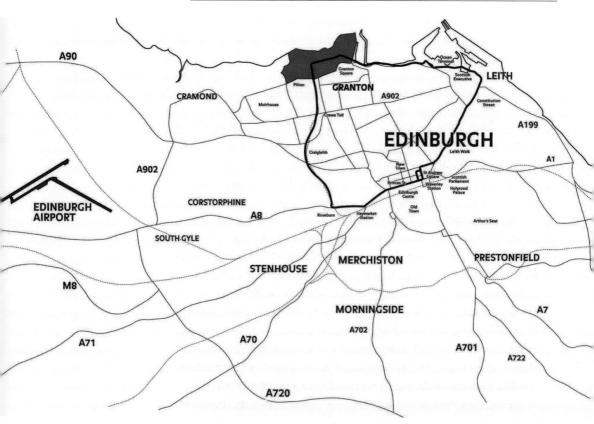

In March 2003, the Scottish Executive committed to provide £190m funding to build the North Edinburgh Tram Loop which will link Granton to the city centre

But the venture goes much further than that. There are also plans for the building of a World Trade Centre, the development of the existing small-scale marina at Granton Harbour, the moving of Telford College to a new campus site within the development area, a new primary school and a tram link with the centre of the city.

Already Waterfront Edinburgh Ltd has been awarded a licence to establish a World Trade Centre (the second in Britain), and the Scottish Executive announced in March 2003 that they would provide £190m funding to construct what is called the North Edinburgh Loop. This new transport initiative will link Granton, clockwise, with Ocean Terminal, Leith Walk, St Andrew Square, Princes Street and Haymarket. It will then head north once more, using the solum of an abandoned railway, towards the development area, and end up back at Granton Square. This is part of a total funding package of £375m announced by the Scottish Executive.

It's an imaginative scheme, and work should start on it by 2005. By 2009 it should be working, each tram carrying a maximum of 250 passengers, and taking 16 minutes for the journey between Granton Square and Princes Street.

The link won't just carry people out of Granton in the morning and return them from their work in the evening. The aim is to integrate the place fully into Edinburgh so that it becomes a destination in its own right. A place to be enjoyed by other city dwellers and by visitors.

Granton over the years has served the people of Edinburgh well. Unlike other parts of the city, it has never loomed large in Scotland's history, though it has had its moments. Rather it has been, over the years, a retreat, a hive of industry, and, thanks to the harbour, a place of trade and commerce. Its new role will retain elements of these, with some additions. It will become a desirable place in which to live and work, and its population will not be drawn from one social stratum.

Vibrant and exciting are perhaps overused words in planning circles nowadays, but they are words that accurately describe a place that has had an honourable past and promises an exciting future.

Day and night artist's impressions of the planned
£16m residential development by the Elphinstone
Group on land sold to them at Granton Harbour by
Forth Property Investments Ltd.

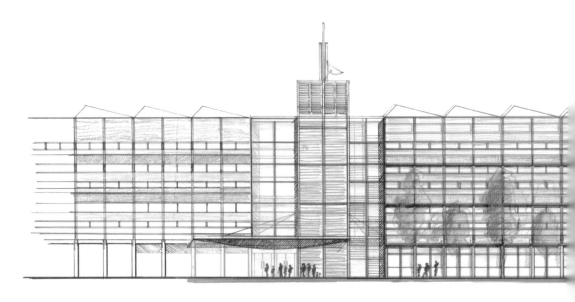

The Elphinstone Group

An artist's impression of the proposed new purpose-built complex for Telford College which is moving to land owned by SecondSite Property. The College has decided to amalgamate its existing four campuses into this single four-storey building. The £30m development will open its doors to students in autumn 2004

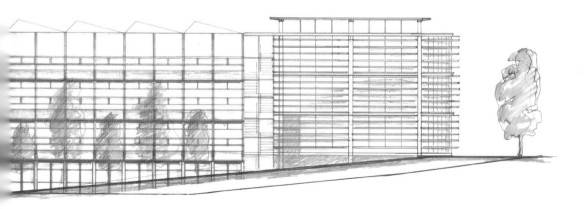

© Keith Brane

© Ken Barry Photography

Index

A

Ainslie Park School 108, 111, 112
Annie Laurie 13, 34, 35
Argyll, Duke of 22, 23, 26

B

British Aerospace Europe 89
Broughton High School 111
Bruce Peebles 90, 92
Buccleuch, Dukes of 12, 23, 27-32, 34, 38, 41, 42, 44, 45, 47, 50, 61, 65-67, 73, 76, 84, 86, 87, 92, 96, 104, 105, 110
Buccleuch, Walter Francis 30, 31, 41

C

Caledonian Railway 67
Caroline Park 12, 21, 22, 23, 24, 27, 28, 29, 32, 33, 34, 35, 36, 37, 49, 67, 86, 87, 91, 97, 104, 105
Caroline Park Foundry 88
Challenger Lodge 95
Church of Scotland 105, 106, 108, 109
Cockburn, Lord 29, 32, 33, 34, 41
Congregational Church 105, 106, 107, 109
Craigmuir School 110, 111
Craigroyston Community High School 111

D

Cramond 17, 18, 22, 28, 38, 105, 110

D

Devlin, TL 52-55, 92

E

Edinburgh City FC 114, 115
Edinburgh, Leith and Granton Railway 66, 67
Edinburgh, Leith and Newhaven Railway 65
Edinburgh Marina Company 62
Edinburgh Street Tramways Company 69
Embassy Cinema 100, 101
esparto grass 56, 85

F

Ferranti 88, 89, 92, 104
Ferranti Thistle 89
ferries 12, 41, 44, 57, 58, 59, 60, 66, 93
fishing fleet 46, 50, 52, 53, 55
AB Fleming & Co 37, 67, 86, 87, 88, 105
flying circus 13, 111
Forth Corinthian Yacht Club 51, 61, 62
Forth Property Investments Ltd 117, 120

G

gasworks 12, 45, 49, 67, 68, 76-80, 84, 87, 88, 97, 117
Gowrie Plot 24

Granton Brick Company 91
Granton Burn 12, 24, 26, 91
Granton Castle 12, 14, 17, 18,
    21, 22, 27, 34, 91
Granton Churches Together 109
Granton Harbour 12, 14-15, 16,
    18, 29, 30, 31, 34, 40, 41,
    45-48, 51, 52, 56, 57, 64-
    68, 73, 84, 91, 111, 119,
    120
Granton House 38, 39
Granton Housing Association 99
Granton Ice Company 91
Granton Parish Church 106
Granton Primary School 110
Granton Quarry 44, 73, 74, 76,
    96
Granton School 105, 110, 111
Granton Square 47, 50, 53, 62,
    70, 93, 94, 105, 106, 110,
    119
Granton Square Bank Robbery
    94
Granton Tavern 50, 93
Granton Township 93
Granton United Church 109
Great Michael 20, 21
Greater Pilton Design Resource
    100

H

HMS Claverhouse
    60, 61, 71, 93

I

Inchview School 110, 111
Industrial Revolution 28, 29, 73

K

Kingsburgh Motor Company 81,
    83

M

Madelvic Motor Carriage Com-
    pany 11, 81, 82, 85, 86
Margaret Paton disaster 54

Methodist Church 107, 109
Muirhouse Festival Association
    100
Murray, Sir John 95, 96
Mushet, Robert ironworks 67, 88

N

National Galleries of Scotland
    104
National Museums of Scotland
    92, 101, 104
Newhaven 12, 13, 20, 21, 41,
    44, 52, 54, 65, 67, 68, 69,
    91
Newhaven Fish Market 52
North Edinburgh Arts 101
Northern General Hospital 112
Northern Lighthouse Board 51,
    84
Northumbria 12, 17, 18

O

Oil and Petroleum 56
Oughton, Sir James 28

P

Parnell, Andrew & Birgitta 37
Peebles Electric Machines 91
Pennywell School 110
Pilton 19, 20, 28, 49, 58, 97,
    99, 100, 115
Pilton Central Association 100
Pirniehall School 110

Q

Quarriers' Cottages 73, 105

R

Roman fort 17
Romans 12, 17
Rough Wooing 13, 18, 19, 21
Royal Forth Yacht Club 51, 61,
    62
Royston Castle 27
Royston House 12,
    24, 25, 26, 27, 37

Royston Mains 97, 108, 109
Royston School 110

S

Salvation Army 106, 107, 109
Scott, Lady 34, 35, 37
Scottish Field 37
Scottish Marine Station 95, 96
SecondSite Property Ltd 117
ship breaker's yard 91
Smith, Alexander 100
St David's School 108, 110, 111
St Margaret Mary's RC Church
    107
Statistical Account 28
Stirling Motor Carriages 83

T

Tarbat, Viscount 25
Telford College 111, 119, 121

trams 69, 70, 71
Triangle Arts Centre 100

U

Union of Parliaments 13, 26, 27
United Wire 83, 85, 86
Urquhart, Fred 100

V

VA Tech Peebles Transformers 90

W

Waterfront Edinburgh Ltd 117,
    119
Welsh, Irvine 100
World Trade Centre 119
World War I 46, 61, 83, 92
World War II 47, 54, 56, 59, 62,
    77, 90, 92, 98, 100, 113,
    115

About the author
James Gracie is a freelance travel/heritage writer who
has written many guidebooks and articles for the
national press. Though not a native of Edinburgh, he
spent many weeks immersed in Granton history,
exploring the area and interviewing its people.
He found it one of the most fascinating projects he has
ever undertaken.